TEACHING ENGLISH AS A SECOND LANGUAGE

C.PAUL VERGHESE

STERLING

STERLING PUBLISHERS (P) LTD.
Regd. Office: A1/256 Safdarjung Enclave, New Delhi-110029.
CIN: U22110DL1964PTC211907
Phone: +91 82877 98380/ +91 120-6251823
e-mail: mail@sterlingpublishers.in
www.sterlingpublishers.in

Teaching English as a Second Language
© 2020, Sterling Publishers Pvt. Ltd.
ISBN 978 81 207 0942 3
First Edition 1990
Tenth Reprint 2009
Reprint 2012, 2013, 2014, 2016, 2020, 2024

Printed in India

Printed and Published by Sterling Publishers Pvt. Ltd.,
Plot No. 13, Ecotech-III, Greater Noida - 201306, Uttar Pradesh, India

PREFACE

This book is intended for students who offer to work on Teaching English as a Second Language as part of their Post-Graduate course in English Language and Literature. It is, therefore, mainly a compilation of facts and findings pertaining to the teaching of English as a second language arrived at by teachers and linguists on the basis of their experience and study. All the same an attempt has been made in the book to put the teaching of English as a Second Language in its proper perspective, define its aims and objectives, and indicate the lines on which the system can be scientifically overhauled and the teaching made effective.

The usefulness of the book, it is believed, also extends to teachers of English who are prepared to accept new ideas and views in an effort to improve their own performance in the interest of their students. The book is by and large free from linguistic jargon and is for this reason useful to the uninitiated but inquisitive general readers who may feel concerned about the prospect of English language teaching.

This book has been written under the University Grants Commission's Scheme for the Preparation of University Level Text-books by Indian Authors. I am, therefore, grateful to the UGC for all the assistance the Commission has extended to me. My thanks are also due to Dr. T.A. George, Principal, Catholicate College, Pathanamthitta, who gave me facilities in the college to work on the project, and to Prof. K. Thankappan Nair, Head of the Department of Hindi, Baselius College, Kottayam for the readiness with which he got me books and materials from the libraries in Trivandrum including the British Council Library, and found time to discuss with me the problem of bilingualism as well as the application of contrastive analysis as a technique in the teaching of English as a Second Language.

Vaikom   C. **Paul Verghese**

CONTENTS

ONE

THE IMPORTANCE OF LEARNING ENGLISH

Of all the languages in the world today English deserves to be regarded as a world language. It is the world's most widely spoken language. It is the common means of communication between the peoples of different nations. One person out of every four on earth can be reached through English. Randolph Quirk points out: "There are now something like 250 million people for whom English is the mother tongue or 'first language'. If we add to this the number of people who have a working knowledge of English as a second or foreign language (many Indians, Africans, Frenchmen, Russians, and so on), we raise the total to about 350 million."[1]

It is true that English is the mother tongue of the people of Great Britain. But they are not the only native speakers of the language. Americans (citizens of the U.S.A.), Canadians and Australians too are native speakers of English. So, English is not the mother tongue of the people of Great Britain only. That is to say, the native speakers of English are not confined to Great Britain, but are spread over three continents of the world, namely, Australia, Europe, and America. To quote Quirk again, "... most people who speak English are not English and were not born in England. Not only has the 'national' sense of English no official political meaning: the 'language' sense of 'English' (importantly, as we shall see) has no necessary link with the genetic sense either."[2].

It is a historical accident that led to English taking deep roots in Canada, Australia and the United States. History again has played a part in English being used widely in other countries in Africa and Asia. These countries were the colonies of Great Britain, and since the day they came under British rule, English has been taught and used as a medium of communication there. In countries like India, Ceylon, Singapore, Pakistan, Nigeria, Zambia, etc., English is still used. In India, for instance, English continues to be the medium of instruction in colleges and universities, and is also the language of administration. The importance of English has been fully realised by the administrators of

India. One of India's Education Commissions has emphatically asserted: "For a successful completion of the first degree course, a student should possess an adequate command of English, be able to express himself with reasonable ease and felicity, understand lectures in it, and avail himself of its literature. Therefore, adequate emphasis will have to be laid on its study as a language right from the school stage. English should be the most useful 'library language' in higher education and our most significant window on the world."[3] What is said here is equally applicable to the other former colonies in Asia and Africa too. And no wonder, English is the medium of instruction as well as the language of administration in a number of Asian and African countries today.

Most of the countries cannot give up the use of English for more than one reason. English education helped them get their ideas on freedom and self-government and enabled them to fight for the independence of their countries. In the multi-lingual contexts of these countries English became a unifying force and helped the freedom-fighters propagate the ideas of nationalism and self-rule. In these countries English still remains a cementing force. For instance, had it not been for the use of the English language, India, multi-lingual as she is, would have had greater constraints to reckon with to remain a united nation.

English, though an adopted language in India, Nigeria, etc., has deep cultural roots in these countries, and has become part and parcel of the intellectual as well as the emotional make-up of the educated people there. Not only has English enriched the languages of these countries, but it has also lent itself to be the medium of creative expression for some of the writers of these countries. Thus in India we have Mulk Raj Anand, R.K. Narayan, Raja Rao and others writing in English, and in Nigeria Chinua Achebe, Wole Soyinka and others. Similarly in the West Indies we have writers like V.S. Naipaul, even as there are great many world-famous writers in English in the erstwhile colonies of Great Britain. The literatures written in English in these countries today constitute what has come to be called Commonwealth English Literature as distinguished from English Literature and American Literature.

A very important reason for regarding English as a world language is that the world's knowledge is enshrined in English. Countries in Asia and Africa that were till recently under the British rule get their scientific knowledge and technological know-how from English books. It is knowledge of English that helps these countries maintain the high level of their intellectual and scientific training and achievement.

Apart from the former British colonies there are other countries like Japan, Korea, etc., in Asia, and some of the European and Latin American countries where also English is taught as a second or third language purely out of utilitarian considerations. That is to say, almost the world over, whether as mother-tongue or as a foreign language, English is being used one way or another. This fact, more than any other, makes English merit the status of a world language. Already English has been accorded this status by the world because it is the language used in international conferences and in the forums of the United Nations Organisation.

English is being learnt and used all over the world not out of any imposition but through the realisation that it has certain inherent advantages. Today the compulsions of learning English are no longer merely political but scientific and technological. And no longer is English the language of Great Britain only; it is the language required by the world for greater understanding, "it is the most *international* of languages."[4]

For over a century and a half Indian intellectuals have been studying English. Today English has entered the fabric of India's culture. The first three decades of the nineteenth century marked the beginning of English education in India, but it was a period of slow incubation. However, the study of English strengthened in the years that followed Macaulay's Minute on Education in India, and with the implementation of the educational policy of Macaulay, a social, cultural and literary renaissance swept over the whole of India. But Macaulay's dream of completely anglicising India mentally and intellectually was not fulfilled; nor did his expectation that Indians would renounce their past history, traditions and culture come true. This was because he had completely ignored the fact that India had an ancient culture and her own heritage besides her having her own languages with their literatures. But the scheme resulted in the adoption of English as the official language of India, and helped to revivify the regional languages. Another and far more important consequence of the use of English was that it stimulated a new consciousness, among the people, of political and cultural nationalism and encouraged the quest for the true meaning of the Indian experience of history in relation to the West. Equally important was the diffusion of Western thought and European liberalism which attracted the great minds of the nineteenth and twentieth centuries in India. The encounter between Eastern and Western thought left a permanent impress on India's cultural history. New movements, religious, social, and cultural also sprang out of this encounter.

The net result of the new system of education thus was that Indian culture without losing its roots received the quick graft of Western ideas which it needed to stay alive. In other words, there was a synthesis of Eastern and Western thought in India's leaders and intellectuals right from the days of Ram Mohun Roy to the present. The prose writings of Tagore, Sri Aurobindo, Mahatma Gandhi, Jawaharlal Nehru and Sarvepalli Radhakrishnan amply illustrate this synthesis. These great sons of modern India not only imbibed Western ideas and thought but also upheld Indian culture and heritage and were able to mould and define the pattern of India's thought and action. Besides, their English writings reveal that each one of them has developed a style of his own which, whether plain or coloured, rhetorical or lucid, eloquent or sensitive, is at once true to the genius of the English language and strikingly *sui generis* and has admirably served the purpose for which it has been employed.

There are today three categories of people in India who want to use English. The first group consists of those who want to use it as an instrument of communication. To the second group belong those who use English as a medium through which they can derive sustenance from the literatures of the West, especially those of England and the U.S.A.; a great deal of Western literature other than that of Great Britain and North America is available to Indians only in English. There is yet a third group of persons, a small minority but perhaps much more important than the other groups that use the English language as a medium of creative exploration and expression of their experience of life.

The increasing use of English for creative expression and the adaptation of the language by writers like Mulk Raj Anand, Bhabani Bhattacharya, Raja Rao etc., in the dialogue in their novels have given rise to the notion of what is called Indian English. Some have even spoken of the evolution of 'Indish', "a common language as the medium of communication and government work in the country"— "a language having the alphabet, the framework and basic structure of English, in the Roman script, an organic language growing freely and assimilating new words, new ideas, new constructions, new idioms, even, if necessary, new letters of the alphabet, from each one of the regional languages of India."[5]

The concept of 'Indish' or 'Indian English' based on the legalisation of the common mistakes made by us using English goes against notions of acceptability and intelligibility. It is true that the kind of English spoken by Indians bears the stamp of their mother tongue, though in some cases an approximation to an acceptable standard exists. But this does not mean that we should have a kind of 'nationalised', 'socialised', 'vernacularised' English. Such an English is sub-standard and not even remotely connected with the creative use of English by some Indian writers.

Braj B. Kachru who has made a study of Indian English in his paper entitled "Indian English: A Study in Contextualisation" contributed to In *Memory of JR. Firth* (1964) says: "In the spoken medium Indian English has by now established itself into an Indian variety of English... Indian English has ramifications in Indian culture (which includes languages) and is used in India towards maintaining appropriate Indian patterns of life, culture and education. This, in short, we might call the Indianness of Indian English, in the same way as we speak of the Englishness of British English." All that Kachru means is that the spoken English of the educated Indian has in it echoes of his social, cultural and linguistic habits. The very fact that he has chosen the dialogue in Indian fiction in English for his linguistic analysis proves one point; the Indian novelists in English have adapted English for portraying the cultural life of a people to whom English is not native and who have their own languages; they have not written their novels with a view to flouting the syntactical and grammatical rules of English. Kachru's emphasis is on Indian English as a creative medium and not as a medium of ordinary communication that has legitimised syntactical and grammatical mistakes.

Perhaps the best definition of 'Indian English' is the one given by V.K. Gokak. According to him 'Indian English' represents "the evolution of a distinct standard a soul the body of which is correct English usage, but whose soul is Indian in colour, thought and imagery, and, now and then, even in the evolution of an Indian idiom which is expressive of the unique quality of the Indian mind while conforming to the 'correctness' of English usage. It is illustrative of a special type of language phenomenon—a language foreign to the people who use it, but accepted by them because of political and, recently cultural reasons."[6] Gokak stresses here the point that our English differs from British English or American English but conforms to the correctness of English usage. Good 'Indian English' is simply good English, English that differs a little in pronunciation, word choice and idiom from good English as written in New York or London. It rests upon the same basis as that which the Standard English of Great Britain rests upon.

For us, Indians, English has a special place. This is not merely because English is a world language but because it has historical associations and has made an impact on our cultural life. For this reason English is not a foreign language to us; it is a second language. It is unlike Russian or French or German to us. So, in the teaching of English in India we should treat it as a second language and not as a foreign language.

Albert H Marckwardt has made a distinction between 'English as a Foreign Language' and 'English as a Second Language'. According to him, when English is "taught as a school subject or on an adult level solely for the purpose of giving the student a foreign-language competence which he may use in one of several ways", then it is taught as a foreign language. But English becomes a second language when it is a language of instruction in schools and colleges and is used as "a lingua franca between speakers of widely diverse languages, as in India."[7] The same distinction is made by D.A. Wilkins when he says: "it is common to use the former (foreign language) to refer to the status of a language which is not used for any normal day-to-day social interaction in the country where it is being learnt, and, by contrast, to use the latter (second language) where, without being the native language of any social group in the country, it is nonetheless used for such purposes as the conduct of commerce, industry, law, administration, politics and education."[8]

We need English not only for operational purposes but also for identifying ourselves with those who use the language in India and abroad. Two main kinds of motivation are at work in our approach to English learning: instrumental and integrative. Geoffrey Broughton and his colleagues who speak of the above two kinds of motivation further say: "When anyone learns a foreign language instrumentally he needs it for operational purposes to be able to read books in the new language, to be able to communicate with other speakers of that language. The tourist, the salesman, the science student are clearly motivated to learn English instrumentally. When anyone learns a foreign language for integrative purposes... he wants to feel at home in it."[9]

There is, however, the fact that inhibits us from teaching English as a second language instead of as a foreign language; this is the decreasing role of English in India. This fact will perhaps make for a shift of emphasis to change from a second language situation to something nearer to a foreign language situation. But the increasing awareness of the importance of English in the world should compel us to learn it for special or specific purposes and for widening our intellectual horizon.

So, our aim in teaching English to our students is to enable them to use English with ease and comfort, that is, to use it both instrumentally and integratively. That is to say, they should be able to speak and write English effectively and develop an ability to understand the basic patterns of the culture of the English-speaking peoples. It is possible for us to realise the aims if we successfully cope with the problems of teaching

English as a second language. Learning English as a foreign language, that is, learning it instrumentally only, will not serve us adequately in our communication within India and with those outside India.

References

1.   Quirk, Randolph, *The Use of English, London: Longman,* 1962, p.8
2.   ibid., p. 2
3.   *Report of the Education Commission,* New Delhi: Ministry of Education, 1966, p.15
4.   Quirk, Randolph, op. cit., p. 5
5.   Raj Kumar's "Presidential Address" at the All-India English Teachers' Conference held at Bhubaneswar in December 1970. For comments on the concept of 'Indish', read C. Paul Verghese's *Essays on Indian Writing in English,* New Delhi, N.V. Publications, pp. 8-13
6.   Gokak, V.K., *The Poetic Approach to Language,* O.U.P., 1952, pp.93-94
7.   Allen, Harold B. (Ed.), *Teaching English as a Second Language: A Book of Readings,* Bombay: McGraw-Hill (reprinted in India), 1965, p.4
8.   Wilkins, D.A., *Second-Language Learning and Teaching,* London: Edward Arnold, 1974, pp. 49-50. See also pp. 150-56 of *Linguistics in Language Teaching,* (London: Edward Arnold, 1980) by D.A. Wilkins
9.   Broughton, Geoffrey & Others, *Teaching English as a Foreign Language,* London: Routledge & Kegan Paul, 1978, p. 5

For Further Reading

1.   Christophersen, P., Second-Language Learning, Harmondsworth: Penguin, 1973
2.   Broughton, Geoffrey & Others, *Teaching English as a Foreign Language,* London: Routledge & Kegan Paul, 1978
3.   Quirk, Randolph, *The Use of English,* London: Longman, 1962
4.   Strevens, P., *New Orientations in the Teaching of English,* O.U.P. 1977
5.   *The Study of English in India,* New Delhi: Ministry of Education, 1967
6.   Gokak, V.K. *English in India: Its Present and Future,* Bombay: Asia Publishing House, 1964

TWO

ENGLISH FOR COMMUNICATION

Language is a means of communicating thoughts and feelings, though not the only means. Cries, signs, gestures, pictorial representations, etc., also serve as a means. Animals other than human beings too communicate with one another. They employ a variety of methods including vocal signals and body movements as well as facial expressions like the baring of teeth. They stimulate one another to action by means of cries. Many birds utter warning calls at the approach of danger; some animals make mating calls. Most of the animals utter cries that are expressive of anger, fear, pleasure, etc. But these modes of communication differ from human language. The sounds or cries made by animals are not articulate. That is to say, they lack the kind of structure that enables us to divide a human utterance into words; a human language is a signalling system which uses vocal sounds and is based on man's ability to speak. The written language is derivative and secondary; it is derived from the spoken language. The basis of language is speech which in turn means the production of meaningful sounds according to a system.

Man alone uses language for communication. As Dwight Bolinger says: "Language is species-specific. It is a uniquely human trait, shared by the cultures so diverse and by individuals physically and mentally so unlike one another..."[1]. Language is one of the most important characteristic forms of human behaviour. It is man's ability to use language for purposes of communication that distinguishes him from other animals. Accordingly, it has always had a place in human affairs.

Man has many achievements to his credit. Science and technology, the conquests and exploration of the normally inaccessible regions of the earth and of outer space, the civilization man has built up so painstakingly, the arts and crafts that form part of this civilization, the global network of communication system, etc., are his noteworthy achievements. But none of them is as great an achievement as his ability to use language; for without the use of language the other achievements would not have been possible. Language, in fact, is the great tool which has made human civilization possible.

Man is often referred to as homo sapiens; this is because he is capable of thinking and of wisdom. Earlier he was homo erectus, and earlier still, he was homo habilis. Homo habilis made stone tools; homo erectus walked aright. But homo sapiens began to think. Language came to his assistance for thinking. No worthwhile thinking leading to sensible and rational conclusions is possible unless one uses language. The most important tool for thinking or ratiocination is language. Without language and ratiocination no great human achievement would have been possible. This perhaps sounds debatable, for psycholinguistics which has raised the question whether or not it is possible to think without language suggests that thought does not depend entirely on language; experiments with young deaf children who lack language skills have shown that they possess the ability to work out certain intellectual problems. Opposed to this is the argument of the American linguist and anthropologist, Benjamin L. Whorf, who says that the words and structures of a person's language control his way of thinking, and ultimately the whole culture to which it belongs. So, the way in which we see the world is, according to Whorf, determined by language. Whatever be the ultimate outcome of a controversy like this, one thing is certain; language does seem to be essential to facilitate thinking processes for anything other than the most simple mental operations and emotional responses.

Human language differs from other modes of communication; it is a system. Edward Sapir explains this aspect of language in his Language: *An Introduction to the Study of Speech;* he says: "Language is a purely human and non-instinctive method of communicating ideas, emotions, and desires by means of a system of voluntarily produced symbols. These symbols are, in the first instance auditory and they are produced by the so-called 'organs of speech'. There is no discernible instinctive basis for human speech as such, however much instinctive tendencies, motor and other, may give a predetermined range or mould to linguistic expression. Such human or animal communication, if 'communication' it may be called, as is brought about by involuntary, instinctive cries is not, in our sense, language at all."[2] Proceeding, Sapir points out that language is a cultural, not a biologically inherited function. In other words, speaking and writing a language are skills that have to be acquired, and are not as instinctive as the biological function of walking. He says: "Walking is an organic, an instinctive function (not, of course, itself an instinct); speech is a non-instinctive, acquired, 'cultural' function."[3]

Capacity for speech is a characteristic of the human race, and of the human race alone. (Perhaps it is better to describe man as homoloquens—man capable of speech—than homo sapiens). As Hockett points out human language has seven characteristics which are not shared by any other communicative system, and this fact makes it unique. These seven characteristics are: duality, productivity, arbitrariness, interchangeability, specialisation, displacement, and cultural transmission. The structure of language is dual as it has a system of significant units of sound (phonemes) and a system of significant units of form (morphemes). By productivity is meant the structural elements of language that enable a speaker to produce new utterances. Language is arbitrary in the sense that there is no inherent or necessary relation between any given feature of a language and its meaning. Interchangeability implies that language as a system can both send and receive messages. Specialisation signifies that the fact that each human language is a special system and has its own framework of structure and meaning and that the system is suitable for conveying messages within the framework. The sixth characteristic, displacement, means that human language can be used both denotatively and connotatively (i.e. extensionally and intentionally) and not only in the direct context to which reference is made but also when the context referred to is absent. Cultural transmission, the seventh characteristic, refers to the fact that "human language is transmitted from one individual to another not by physical inheritance, but by learning."[4]

Of the above seven characteristics the two fundamental ones are productivity and duality or structural complexity. Our faculty of language enables us to utter sentences which have never been constructed by us previously and many of which have never been constructed by anyone else either. We can, in other words, communicate in a limitless variety of ways using the language we have acquired from our environment. By the use of the term, duality, Hockett implies only the meaningful arrangements of phonemes and morphemes. So, his concept of duality in respect of language is based on the structure of the language as well as on its semantic properties. That is to say, the highly structured system of language enables us to communicate our thoughts in a variety of ways. Geoffrey Broughton and his colleagues explain the concept thus: "Communication can be infinitely varied and infinitely complex just because language is a highly structured system which allows an infinite range of permutations. The structure is of many types: the organisation of a fixed range of sounds, the ordering of words in phrases and sentences, the use of inflections, the semantic and grammatical relationships between words, the interplay of stress, intonation and rhythm in the actual production of speech, and the dovetailing of paralinguistic features."[5]

The purpose of language, as we have seen, is communication, which means that language helps a person formulate his thought and encode it for the benefit of others who decode it. Encoding and decoding take place virtually simultaneously. This is because both the sender and the receiver of the code are familiar with the vocal sounds, the words and phrases which these sounds constitute, the structural arrangements of the words and phrases, their semantic import, etc.

The native speaker of a language has grown up with the language and does not have any difficulty in encoding and decoding the message uttered in the language. In other words he has the ability to produce an infinite number of potential sentences in the language remaining within its own framework of structure and meaning. (This ability of the native speaker varies from person to person depending on his conscious striving and training to master the language.) The framework itself is governed by a finite set of rules. The aim of learning a second language, say English, is to achieve the same linguistic competence that the native speaker of the language possesses. As F.S. Scott and his colleagues say in their *English Grammar: A Linguistic Study of Its Classes and Structures:* "To learn another language is not merely to learn a new set of sounds or marks on paper for saying something, it is to learn that it is possible to think in a slightly different way from that to which one has become used, to understand that there is more than one way of organising our experience and that the world is a rather greater place than one once thought."[6] What this in effect means is that when we learn English we should aim at a degree of language proficiency, both in speech and in writing, that is comparable to the native speaker's. In other words, we should be able to express ourselves in English in the right ways on the right occasions. It is the nature of the occasion that determines what kind of formal or informal language will be most appropriate. For informal occasions we should be able to use informal English, and for the formal ones, a more formal version of normal, customary English.

A mere ability to use the linguistic forms correctly will not do; we should be able to use them appropriately. According to Robert Lado, "Learning a second language is... acquiring the ability to use its structure within a general vocabulary under essentially the conditions of normal communication among native speakers at conversational speed." He further says: "...it means the acquisition of the ability to use, in speaking, the units and patterns of expression of the second language associated with the units and patterns of content when listening to the second language. It means, in other words, learning the expression, the content and their association for rapid use in the proper positions within the system of the target language."[7]

English, as already mentioned in the first chapter, is the best second language suited for us in India for historical and other reasons. But the question arises: what variety of English should we learn? The question is important because there are varieties of English, global, regional, historical, geographical, social etc. Of the global varieties of English American English and British English are the principal ones. Perhaps the differences between the two are highly exaggerated at the expense of the overwhelming similarity and the underlying unity between the two forms of English. In actual fact, the similarity between the two is quite evident in their having a common inflectional system and syntax. The differences are to be found chiefly in a few features of pronunciation and in certain sectors of vocabulary. The framework or skeleton of the standard language is basically the same in British and American English.

The different varieties of English are called dialects. Dialects are differentiated on the basis of grammar, vocabulary, pronunciation and speech habits. The difference between American and British (or Australian) English mentioned above is geographical and can be termed as dialects in a wider sense. Regional dialects also come under geographical dialects. Geographical dialects arise out of a vertical division of the speakers of the same language. Other divisions which have given rise to dialects are regarded as horizontal; these are educational, social, occupational, etc. Jargon is an example of occupational dialect. Dialectal variations are acceptable to the group of people who speak the dialect and are largely confined to spoken language. For purposes of writing, almost all attempt to use a standard language. What is called bad grammar in the case of the native speaker arises from dialectal variations. As Randolph Quirk points out, "...the greater part of English is common to all dialects, educational levels and styles: such grammar is clearly within the range of what can be called Standard English." He further adds: "But we see also that there are some grammatical features which distinguish one dialect from another within Great Britain, or which distinguish British from American usage, or which distinguish formal from colloquial and colloquial from uneducated usage. There is one other thing that is important for us to see. The major regional distinctions (between British and American usage in particular) do not over-ride others."[8]

What is important to note here is that there is a Standard English which is the basis of all varieties of English—these varieties include all kinds of dialects and registers, colloquial speech and slang. We may call this 'neutral English' as E.V. Gatenby does in his article in Vol. II No.3 of "Teaching of English". Gatenby says-: "The modern requirement is a neutral form of English as free from national bias as Esperanto...Starting with neutral English and adapting it, if necessary, to a particular region is a very different process from starting with English of Oxford and removing its cultural flavour to fit it for *en tout cas* use."

Gatenby's suggestion is based on his belief that in India and other erstwhile British colonies learning English in the ways the Britishers want it will be resisted. What he means by neutral English is "any mutually intelligible form of educated English" which "is universally acceptable". That is to say, neutral English is Standard English which is acceptable for international communication. Any regional standard (Indian English may be regarded as a regional standard) becomes acceptable when it divests itself of those local peculiarities that hamper international communication. Randolph Quirk observes: "Standard English is, as Lawrence's Hilda put it, 'normal English'; that kind of English which draws least attention to itself over the widest area and through the widest range of usage. (As we have seen), this norm is a complex function of vocabulary, grammar, and transmission, most clearly established in one of the means of transmission (spelling), and least clearly established in the other means of transmission (pronunciation). This latter point draws attention to one important factor in the notion of a standard, it is particularly associated with English in a *written* form, and we find that there are sharper restrictions in every way upon the English that is written (and especially *printed*) than upon English that is spoken. In fact, the standards of Standard English are determined and preserved, to no small extent, by the great printing houses... Standard English is basically an ideal, a mode of expression that we seek when we wish to communicate beyond our immediate community, English-speakers as a whole. As an ideal, it cannot be perfectly realised, and we must expect that members of different 'wider communities' (Britain, America, Nigeria, for example) may produce different realisations. In fact, however, the remarkable thing is the very high degree of unanimity, the small amount of divergence. Any of us can read a newspaper printed in Leeds or San Francisco or Delhi without difficulty and often even without realising that there are differences at all."[9]

This means that there is what may be called a Standard English and that it is acceptable and intelligible to the English speakers as a whole. The basis of this standard "is the very high degree of unanimity, the small amount of divergence." That is to say, intelligibility and acceptability, both in spoken and written English, are the basic requirements. Perfectionists may disagree; they may say that this is a kind of easy tolerance of mistakes that will pave the way for 'bad' English. But then they must be able to define 'good' English from the Indian student's point of view. In the absence of a convincing definition of 'good' English (especially in view of the vast varieties of English, and of variations based on numerous dialects and registers) if we try to teach all the refinements of pronunciation, intonation, stress, etc., we shall end by teaching nothing thoroughly. To achieve success our objectives should be limited. Our attempt, while teaching English as a second language, must be to find out how international intelligibility and acceptability suffer on account of the interference of regional languages and their pressures on the Indian learners of English, and to eliminate these pressures to the extent possible.

Intelligibility, both in spoken and written English, is the very first requirement. Speakers with an excellent understanding and command of syntax and lexis may be grossly unintelligible because they have a poor command of the phonology of the language. Since the phonological system is the smallest of the three systems, an earnest attempt can be made by Indian teachers of English to train their students in proper articulation. It may be remembered that the qualities of the sounds made by native speakers are immensely variable and that consequently, they and, even the experienced foreign speakers, have great tolerance for wide variations in the pronunciation of the same phonological unit. Pronunciation of 'coat', for example, as/ko:t/instead of/kout/does not damage intelligibility in the least. But intelligibility suffers because of confusion between sounds with meaningful contrasts (e.g., /ship/v./sheep/), intrusion of extraneous sounds because of distributional features of the mother-tongue (e.g./isku:1/for/sku: 1/or failure to aspirate initial /p/, /t/, or /k/ Misapplications of lexis and idiom also damage or destroy intelligibility in speech and writing. Unintelligibility occurs when what is meant to be understood is not understood.

What is intelligible may not, however, be acceptable. For example, 'We are provided good accommodation for our stay in Trivandrum' or 'Where you are going?' is intelligible but not acceptable. Acceptability is much harder to determine than intelligibility. An exact border-line between acceptability and unacceptability is quite impossible to draw. Broadly speaking, an intelligible utterance may be said to be unacceptable when the recipient reader or listener is led to believe that the writer or speaker is to a marked degree (i) socially inferior (e.g. 'They was a bloody good set of chaps'—an utterance which thousands of native speakers might produce),

(ii) educationally inferior (e.g. 'You've known him quite well, isn't it?'—an utterance which will deeply offend educated native as well as non-native speakers of English), or (iii) ludicrous (e.g. 'Please, go to the backside of the house' or 'I beg to apply for leave because my venerated and deceased father has, alas, bade farewell eternally to this mortal coil') because of inaccuracies, inappropriateness, etc. The acceptability of an intelligible utterance is very much a matter of its appropriateness to the norms of the listener or reader, set of listeners or readers to whom it is addressed. Hence acceptability takes us outside the limits of most grammar books and most linguistic studies.

In his monograph entitled *The Intelligibility of Indian English* R.K. Bansal makes the point that even within India there are a large number of regional varieties of English and that each one is different from the other in certain ways because of the pressure of the Indian language spoken in a particular region. These regional varieties are at times not even mutually intelligible. But, Bansal also notes that "there are people who have shaken off the gross features of regional accent and speak a more 'neutral' form of Indian English." He adds: "English as spoken by educated people in India does not differ radically from native English in grammar and vocabulary, but in pronunciation it is different from both British and American English... It is also true that in every region there are good speakers of English and bad speakers of English."[10]

The point is that teaching English as a second language in India should aim at international intelligibility which can be realised by getting rid of regional peculiarities of pronunciation, accent and syntax and by a sincere striving for grammatical correctness. In the learning of English in India the habits that one has already acquired along with the acquisition of one's language persist and stand as an impediment in the way of learning a whole set of new habits of speech while acquiring a second language. One has, therefore, to keep always in mind the fact that each language has a different system and that while learning a second language or a foreign language one has to follow the system of the language.

Now that we have defined intelligibility and acceptability in the Indian context we may ask the question what exactly should be the aims of teaching English in India. The basic aim of teaching any second language is to enable the student to develop the skills of speaking, listening, reading, and writing. It is while speaking and writing that the problem of intelligibility and acceptability arises. Here too the question of pronunciation, grammar, usage and vocabulary comes in. Correctness based on internationally accepted standards cannot be ignored by us; for today the compulsions of learning English in India are no longer merely political and national but scientific, technological and international. Teachers of English should, therefore, undertake the task of giving a sound knowledge of English to our students keeping in mind a radically enlarged view of the function of English in India as well as in the world today. The emphasis ought to be on good English and not on English just as 'a library language' or as a language a working knowledge of which can help get information and knowledge from books written in English without having the ability to use the language for intelligent discussion and communication. So, we cannot dispute that the Indian student must learn the grammar of English in the sense that the sentences he produces must conform to English patterns in the accepted model; nor can we dispute that his speech habits should be intelligible and acceptable enough to suit the occasions for which his utterances are intended.

Generally speaking, there are five functions which communication ought to achieve. First, there is the personal function of revealing oneself; then, there is the direct utterance in which one attempts to control the listener; a third one is what the anthropologist Bronislaw Malinowski calls 'phatic communion' which means establishing relationship by speaking in a ritualised way.[11] Yet another function of language is seen in the referential utterance in which information is conveyed to listeners. Last, there is the creative use of language as in poetry, songs, etc. If English has to be used for communication by an Indian student, he should achieve the competence to suit the language to the occasion and also to listen with understanding to other speakers and interpret them to the full. Geoffrey Broughton and his colleagues are right when they observe: "As far as the foreign learner is concerned, the history of language teaching shows emphasis on a very limited range of competence which has been called 'classroom English' or 'textbook English', and has often proved less than useful for any 'real' communicative purpose. That is to say, as long as the use of English as a foreign language was confined to largely academic purposes, or to restricted areas like commerce or administration, a limited command of the language chiefly in the written form, was found reasonable and adequate. But in modern times, the world has shrunk and in many cases interpersonal communication is now more vital than academic usage. It is now important for the learner to be equipped with the command of English which allows him to express himself in speech or in writing in a much greater variety of contexts."[12] What is required is that we in India should lay greater emphasis on the communication needs of our students while teaching them English as a second language.

References

1. Bolinger, Dwight, *Aspects of Language,* New York: Harcourt, Brace & World Inc., 1968, p.3
2. Sapir, Edward, *Language: An Introduction to the Study of Speech,* Herts: Grenada Publishing Ltd., 1970, p. 8
3. ibid., p. 4
4. Cited in *Introductory Linguistics* by Robert A Hall, Delhi: Motilal Banarasidas, 1969 (Indian edition), p.6
5. Broughton, Geoffrey & Others, op. cit., p. 26
6. Scott, F.S. & Others, *English Grammar: A Linguistic Study of Its Classes & Structures,* London: Heinemann Educational Books, 1973, pp. 3-4
7. Lado, Robert, *Language Teaching: A Scientific Approach,* Bombay: Tata McGraw-Hill, 1983 (Indian edition), p. 38
8. *The Use of English,* pp. 98-99
9. *ibid.,* pp. 99-100
10. Bansal, R.K., The *Intelligibility of Indian English,* CIE Monograph No. 4, Madras: Orient Longman, 1966, pp. 38-39
11. Cited in Quirk's *The Use of English,* p. 62. Quirk observes: "He (Malinowski) called this use of language 'phatic communion', and by the term he sought to distinguish that part of our speech behaviour which is given over to polite sociabilities, greetings, empty catch-phrases and the like, which we hear breezily passed around by people in the street or on buses or in casual cafe conversation..."
12. *Teaching English as a Foreign Language,* p. 35

For Further Reading

1. Carroll, J.B., *The Study of Language,* New York, Harvard University Press, 1959
2. Miller, George A., *Language and Communication,* New York: McGraw-Hill, 1951
3. Skinner, B.F., *Verbal Behaviour,* New York: Appleton-Century-Crofts, 1957
4. Wilkins, D.A., *Second-Language Learning and Teaching,* London: Edward Arnold, 1974
5. Widdowson, H.G., *Teaching Language as Communication,* O.U.P., 1978

THREE

PROBLEMS OF THE SECOND-LANGUAGE LEARNER

We, Indians, are not native speakers of English; to us English is a second language. So, learning it is not as natural to us as it is to the native speaker. The native speaker of English has imbibed the language with his mother's milk; he has become familiar with the components of English in the natural process of growing up. This cannot be so with us. For us learning English is essentially a deliberate effort at developing a command and control of the different components of the language; its phonology (the sound system), its morphology (the patterns and parts of words) and its syntax (the patterns of phrases and sentences). The question is: how can we Indians, master these components of English when we learn it as a second language?

There is very little that is known for certain about language learning. All the same we know that the native speaker acquires his mother tongue through imitation and that this is the natural process of language acquisition. Perhaps the conditions under which a child acquires his mother tongue will serve as a clue to the understanding of the process of language learning.

From the moment of his birth the child is exposed to the sounds of the language. He is thus in constant contact with these sounds for most of his waking hours. And most of the language he hears is directed at him by other people. Objects and actions in the surroundings are described to the child in an oversimplified language at first, and later in explanatory utterances. All this results in his 'producing' the language. Perhaps the child also spends many hours in monologues and imaginary dialogues. He is stimulated in this by the language that he is exposed to. Without any conscious effort he learns the essential components of his language. The two significant factors in this process of language acquisition are that the child is exposed to spoken language and that he hears linguistically uncontrolled language. In other words, it is natural speech with all its distortions, omissions and inconsistencies that he hears. Even then he intuits syntactic rules consistent with the formal structure of his language.

A very important aspect of language acquisition is that the child learns whatever language he is expected to. Normally a child is exposed to one language only. If he is exposed to two languages because of his growing up in a bilingual environment, he acquires both languages simultaneously. Though in the early stage there may be a merging of the two languages, later they are separated.

The process of intuiting syntactic rules and the attempt to imitate intonation, pronunciation, etc., enable the child to acquire certain patterns —be they in sounds or in words—when he begins to speak. Not only does he use in his utterances words and phrases that he has heard but he also makes his own verbs or nouns or goes in for abbreviations regardless of their correctness. Quite unconsciously he discovers that there is a grammatical system at work in the utterances he has heard. His own utterances are framed on the basis of this awareness. He makes mistakes, and later discovers where he has gone wrong in the application of the rules of the language he has become aware of. In this process of discovery he is helped by the grown-ups. They sometimes repeat his faulty utterance in a grammatical form and thus indirectly help in the correction. This is a kind of feedback leading to the child's awareness of his mistake. The encouragement given to the child by the grown-ups also acts as a stimulus to his language acquisition. By the age of five the child acquires a substantial proportion of the grammatical system of his language; that is to say, he internalizes most of the grammar of his language.

What we learn from the child's language acquisition process is that exposure to language enables the child to internalize the grammar of his language. The child's exposure is to situations evoking his behaviour, his motivation, instant rewards for success, etc.; also, the world of the child is a linguistic world unhampered by the kind of distractions to which adults learning a second language are subject. Can we then equate the process of language acquisition, which is natural, with that of language learning, which is deliberate and determined?

To answer this question we should know whether the same psychological problems are at work both in language acquisition and in language learning. We have noticed that the child exposed to a language picks it up easily and quickly. But does an adult too acquire a language easily and quickly when exposed to it? Generally it is observed that when children and adults experience the same bilingual situation, children learn the new language more quickly. This in itself does not, however, mean that adults are not as good at acquiring a new language as children. Adults lag behind because they are rarely wholly cut off from the use of their mother tongue;

also, the social pressures on children mixing frequently with those of their age group are more intense than those on adults who can manage with their first language.

It is perhaps true that children acquire a better mastery of pronunciation system than adults; this is because adults who have already an excellent command of their first language cannot easily adapt themselves to the sound system of a new language. But adults learning a second language show better learning abilities than children acquiring a language in that the former have well-developed faculties and can bring to bear deductive and analytical approaches on language learning. The actual achievement of adults is superior to that of children because of their mental faculties that have been developed in the general process of education. Geoffrey Broughton and his colleagues are right when they say: "Adults learning English bring to the task a mature personality, many years of educational training, a developed intelligence, a determination to get what they want, fairly clear aims, and above all strong motivation to make as rapid a progress as possible. These are formidable qualifications which far outweigh any disadvantages, and make teaching adults a challenging and satisfying experience."[2]

One thing is certain; both children and adults learn languages when exposed to them. So, one of the important conditions of learning a second language is abundant exposure to the language. What we find is that the learners of a second language are not as much and as constantly exposed to the language they attempt to learn as a child acquiring his mother tongue. As D.A. Wilkins observes, "One year in the classroom provides the equivalent of from one to three weeks' contact in a language- acquisition situation." He adds: "If it takes from three to four years for a child to learn his mother tongue to a reasonable degree of proficiency, we can work out for ourselves the astronomical length of time it would take for language learning to reach the same level if it was based on the same kind of largely random exposure to language."[3]

The remedy Wilkins suggests is exposure of the second-language learner to linguistic forms in a well-regulated, restricted manner instead of to diverse forms at the same time. He says-: "A succession of linguistically-structured units might well be more effective overall than similar quantity of random material." To restrict or organise exposure in this way, he believes, is an effective way of "facilitating the process of inducing the grammatical system from the language data to which he is exposed."[4]

When exposed to linguistic patterns, it is advisable that the learner is introduced to certain linguistic rules. This is useful in the case of adults because their analytical abilities will help them make the patterns on their own. (Children learning a second language will not, however, benefit by linguistic rules. This is because of ill-developed analytical abilities.) While introducing the learner to linguistic rules, care should be exercised so that learning the rules does not become the main language activity. Any unusual insistence on grammaticality and correct usage is likely to make the learner overcautious and sensitive about committing mistakes. And to this extent his speech becomes inhibited. Exposure to carefully-controlled language should also be accompanied by opportunities for the learner to meet the language in all its diversity so that he becomes familiar with its structural range.

If exposure to language enables the learner to become acquainted with linguistic structures, opportunities to use these structures, if made available to him, will make it possible for him to speak the language closely imitating the teacher and those others who speak the language. Without these opportunities the learner will not be able to gain an effective control of the language. Perhaps he will make mistakes in his utterances, especially in the beginning, but these mistakes will become useful to him if he gets the feedback that enables him to learn from them. Here too the situation is similar to the one in which the child acquiring a language depends on feedback. In the case of the second-language learner the feedback should be the responsibility of the teacher. The teacher's correction of mistakes through the feedback should be cautiously and sympathetically carried out so that the learner does not become self-conscious about making mistakes in his utterances.

A very significant factor in language learning is motivation. The child acquiring his mother tongue has his motivation in the recognition that he wins all around in the urge to establish identity with other children. But the second-language learner has his motivation in the need to communicate—whatever be the level of communication he wants to reach. So, emphasis should be laid on the communicative use of language. The classroom activity should be geared to this, and the learners should be well-motivated to ensure effective learning through a natural urge to communicate.

The second-language learner attaches significance to the meaning of his utterances much more than the child who is in the process of acquiring his mother tongue. This is because of his need to communicate in the language. So, learning becomes more effective when he is drilled in sentence patterns in which he understands every lexical item. It is a well- known fact that what is learned is better retained when the language involved is meaningful. According to Wilkins there are two aspects of this meaningfulness. He says: "First, the wider the range of associations that is built up for the linguistic forms the better... The wider and richer the network of associations that any form possesses for the learner, the less the likelihood of that form being forgotten. Secondly, the learning of sentences that are semantically and structurally well formed, sentences whose meaning and grammatical structure are easily acceptable to the learner, is easier and more permanent than the learning of sentences that are deviant in any way."[5]

The child learns to speak first; then only does he learn to write, and that too when taught; speaking he does without being formally trained. On the analogy of the child's language acquisition, should the second-language learner be taught speech first and writing next? In other words, is it psychologically necessary or beneficial for speech to be learnt before writing? The history of human language shows that it came to be spoken first and written afterwards. This primacy of speech makes linguists argue that the language learner should be trained in listening and speaking first and reading and writing next. But we should not forget that the second- language learner has already learnt his mother tongue and has reached an age at which he can learn what he sees and hears. So, we may not go the whole hog with the linguists; we may make use of both modalities—speech and writing-simultaneously in our scheme of second-language learning.

There are certain variable factors which are of great importance in second-language learning. The most important of these factors is the duration of exposure to the language. In India English is taught as a second language in schools and colleges for five or six hours in a week. Perhaps the duration is hardly adequate; also the courses are spread over years. These two facts make it difficult for us to create a sustained interest and inculcate a sense of progress and achievement in our students. The redeeming feature, however, is that the long period of exposure to English, though intermittent and not intensive, enables our students to have a certain degree of familiarity with sentence patterns, words, and phrases in the language which, with some more continuous contact with the language strengthens his ability to write it though not to speak it.

Another factor in learning is classroom conditions. These conditions include the number of students in a class, the physical arrangements for the class, teaching materials such as chalk, blackboard, audio-visual aids, library etc. It is very important that second-language classes are of the right size. A class consisting of forty or thereabouts becomes unwieldy, and no individual attention can be paid to students. One of the reasons why teaching English in India does not leave the desired impact on the student is that the class is too big for the teacher to do any worthwhile job.

The availability of the right type of teaching materials and audio- visual aids can certainly make the teaching of English in India quite effective. Audio-visual aids are an integral part of the learning situation and are as important as the blackboard and chalk. In India teaching English suffers as a result of the inadequacy and poor availability of these resources. Though English learning begins in the Fourth Standard (in the non-English medium schools in most of the States) and goes on till the end of the Second Year of College education, yet the standard of English reached by students in general is poor. This is because of inadequacies relating to teaching aids and other environmental factors.

The two vital factors in a second-language learning situation are the student and the teacher. The teacher has problems to tackle when he is faced with the task of teaching a class of students who show varying capacities of assimilation. In India even at the college level a large number of students have to be given elementary lessons in the language; they as well as the students who have a better standard feel that the lessons and methods adopted are not appropriate to their age or status. The result is a kind of general resentment. In such circumstances the teacher will have to convince the students that what he wants to do is in their own interests. Some of the students are weakly motivated owing to their social and family background; here the teacher must himself stimulate and sustain motivation. The variations that exist in the standards of students in the same class pose other problems too. Individual attention to students can remedy the situation to a great extent. But this is possible only if the class is of small size. A study of the entry behaviour of each and every student is not practicable; nor is it possible because of the difficulties that come in the way of deciding on objectives in terms of desired terminal behaviour in each of the four skills. What is perhaps possible is to assess the average competence of the class and then to impart systematic instruction taking into account the length of course in terms of teaching time, time at the disposal of the student for personal work, amount of exposure to English outside its study as a subject in its own right, the size of class, availability of books, teaching aids, etc.

Like the student the teacher himself is a variable factor in the scheme of teaching a second language; his skill and personality are instrumental in creating the necessary conditions for learning. He should be proficient in the language; his knowledge of and expertise in methods and techniques of language teaching should be of a reasonably high standard. As Robert Lado says: "The language teacher must be educated, at least to the levels of his peers. He must have the general preparation of a teacher... (He) must know the target language well enough to be imitated by his students."[6] The teacher's language is the principal model for the student. In India the main problem is to have competent teachers of English. A large number of the present teachers are relatively ill-taught and are noted for their lack of professional skill in their understanding of language and language learning and in their command of methods and techniques of language teaching. Wilkins is right when he observes: "It should be unrealistic to expect a teacher to set objectives which he himself is not capable of reaching. A teacher who himself has difficulty in speaking the language he teaches is not going to succeed in giving his pupils a command of spoken language."[7]

A very important pre-requisite for teaching a second language is the availability of competent teachers. Perhaps it is this fact that has impelled the Modern Language Association of America to publish a set of qualifications under seven heads and three levels of excellence under each head. The MLA qualifications are reproduced below:

I. AURAL UNDERSTANDING

(1) *Superior:* Ability to follow closely and with ease all types of standard speech, such as rapid or group conversation, plays, and movies.
(2) *Good:* Ability to understand conversation of average tempo, lectures, and news broadcasts.
(3) *Minimal:* Ability to get the sense of what an educated native says when he is enunciating carefully and speaking simply on a general subject.

II. SPEAKING

(1) *Superior:* Ability to approximate native speech in vocabulary, intonation, and pronunciation (e.g., the ability to exchange ideas and to be at ease in social situations).
(2) *Good:* Ability to talk with a native without making glaring mistakes, and with a command of vocabulary and syntax sufficient to express one's thoughts in sustained conversation.

This implies speech at a normal speed with good pronunciation and intonation.

(3) *Minimal:* Ability to talk on prepared topics (e.g., for classroom situations) without obvious faltering, and to use the common expressions needed for getting around in a foreign country, speaking with a pronunciation readily understandable to a native.

III. READING

(1) *Superior:* Ability to read, almost as easily as in (one's mother tongue), material of considerable difficulty, such as essays and literary criticism.

(2) *Good:* Ability to read with immediate comprehension prose and verse of average difficulty and mature content.

(3) *Minimal:* Ability to grasp directly (i.e., without translating) the meaning of simple, nontechnical prose, except for an occasional word.

IV. WRITING

(1) *Superior:* Ability to write on a variety of subjects with idiomatic naturalness, ease of expression, and some feeling for the style of the language.

(2) *Good:* Ability to write a simple "free composition" with clarity and correctness in vocabulary, idiom and syntax.

(3) *Minimal:* Ability to write correctly sentences or paragraphs such as would be developed orally for classroom situations, and to write a short simple letter.

V. LANGUAGE ANALYSIS

(1) *Superior:* Ability to apply knowledge of descriptive, comparative, and historical linguistics to the language teaching situation.

(2) *Good:* A basic knowledge of the historical development and present characteristics of the language, and an awareness of the difference between the language as spoken and as written.

(3) *Minimal:* A working command of the sound patterns and grammar patterns of (English) and a knowledge of its main differences from (one's mother tongue).

VI. CULTURE

(1) *Superior:* An enlightened understanding of the (English) people and their culture, achieved through personal contact, preferably by travel and residence abroad, through study of systematic descriptions of the (English) culture, and through study of literature and arts.

(2) *Good:* Firsthand knowledge of some literary masterpieces, an understanding of the principal ways in which the (English) culture resembles and differs from (one's) own, and possession of an organised body of information on the (English) people and their civilization.

(3) *Minimal:* An awareness of language as an essential element among the learnt and shared experiences that combine to form a particular culture, and a rudimentary knowledge of the geography, history, literature, art, social customs, and the contemporary civilization of the (English) people.

VII. PROFESSIONAL PREPARATION

(1) *Superior:* A mastery of the recognised teaching methods, and the ability to experiment with and evaluate new methods and techniques.

(2) *Good:* The ability to apply knowledge of methods and techniques to the teaching situation (e.g., audio-visual techniques) and to relate one's teaching of the language to other areas of the curriculum.

(3) *Minimal:* Some knowledge of effective methods and techniques of language teaching.[8]

Every second-language teacher has a serious problem to cope with in the student's bilingualism. In India this problem is more linguistic than social or cultural. Actually, the social and cultural context is in favour of English learning; for a command of English, not a smattering of it, is regarded as the hallmark of an educated person in India. But it is a linguistic problem in so far as the habits of speech in the first language, its syntactical structures, its phonological system, etc., can become impediments to the learning of English. For example, a Hindi speaking student is likely to say, "Though I gave the examination, yet I failed," on the analogy of the linguistic pattern with which he is already familiar in his first language. This is apart from the interference of the phonological system of his mother tongue in his accent, intonation and pronunciation.[9] These impediments can, however, be got over through sustained remedial teaching.

Teaching English as a second language in India is thus beset with problems such as poor motivation, inadequate exposure to the language, poor classroom conditions, lack of teaching aids and materials, incompetence of teachers, bilingualism and its effects on the learner, etc. However, some worthwhile teaching is possible if the right relationship is established in the attitudes of the learner, the teacher, the learner's parents, and if, through this relationship, the learner is properly motivated.

References

1. "Language acquisition' should be distinguished from 'language learning". "Language acquisition' refers to the natural process of acquiring a language, say, one's mother tongue; 'language learning' means learning a second language or a foreign language.
2. *Teaching English as a Foreign Language,* p. 187
3. *Second-Language Learning and Teaching,* pp. 31-32
4. ibid., p. 32
5. ibid., p. 39
6. *Language Teaching: A Scientific Approach,* p. 8
7. op. cit., p. 54
8. Cited in Robert Lado's *Language Teaching: A Scientific Approach* (pp. 230-32). The MLA qualifications have been prepared with the American teacher in mind. Therefore, some minor changes have been made in the text reproduced to suit the Indian context. Brackets indicate the substituted words.
9. The second part of Wallace E. Lambert's essay entitled "Psychological Approaches to the Study of Language" in *Teaching English as a Second Language* (edited by Harold B. Allen) deals with bilingualism. (See pp. 45-50).

For Further Reading

1. Allen, Harold B., (Ed.), *Teaching English as a Second Language,* Bombay, Tata McGraw-Hill, 1965 (revised edition), pp. 8-48
2. Brooks, Nelson, *Language and Language Learning: Theory and Practice,* New York: Harcourt, Brace and World Inc., 1964
3. Fries, Charles C., *Teaching and Learning English as a Foreign Language,* Ann Arbor: The University of Michigan Press, 1945
4. Gauntlett, J.O., *Teaching English as a Foreign Language,* London: Macmillan & Co., 1957
5. Gurrey, P., *Teaching English as Foreign Language,* London: Longman, 1955
6. Ure, J.M. & Velayudhan, S., (Eds.), *Perspectives on English Language Teaching.* Madras: Macmillan, 1985

FOUR

LINGUISTICS AND THE SECOND-LANGUAGE TEACHER

Whether or not linguistics is relevant to the teaching of English as a second language in India is a significant question. This is because "there are those who talk of the 'linguistic method' of language teaching as if to oppose some hypothetical 'non-linguistic method' used in the benighted past."[1] William G. Moulton rightly observes: "Linguistics is not a teaching method, but a growing body of knowledge and theory; and though it may offer helpful answers to some of the problems of language teaching, it surely does not know all the answers."[2] What he means is that linguistics did not originate as a tool in the hands of the language teacher; nor has it aimed at language as its goal. Wilkins makes the point very clear when he says: "It would be absurd to pretend that no one can be a good language teacher unless he has a knowledge of linguistics. It is possible that linguistics is not even one of the most important elements in the preparation of a language teacher. The value of linguistics is that by increasing his awareness of language, it makes him more competent and therefore a better language teacher."[3]

Linguistics is a science, a systematic body of knowledge and theory. Charles C. Fries defines "linguistics or linguistic science as a body of knowledge and understanding concerning the nature and functioning of human language, built up out of information about the structure, the operation, and the history of a wide range of very diverse human languages by means of those techniques and procedures that have proved most successful in establishing verifiable relationship among linguistic phenomena."[4] What follows from this definition is that linguistics is an autonomous discipline and that it is not about language teaching. But both linguistics and language teaching are concerned with language. So, it only stands to reason that each can learn something from the other.

Once it is admitted that linguistics is a body of knowledge and understanding we may legitimately ask the question what contribution the systematic study of languages can make towards the teaching of English as a second language. That is to say, the question with us is: how linguistics can be made useful to second-language teaching. Answers to this question and the earlier question (with which we have started this chapter) depend on our ascertaining the linguist's attitudes towards language.

The linguist believes in the primacy of speech. Though he makes a study of the spoken and written 'forms or modes' of a language, his preference is for the spoken mode. This is because he believes that the relationship between speech and writing is not identical, that speech has preceded writing, and that writing is an attempt to represent the language that is spoken. The linguist's insistence on the primacy of speech is opposed to the old and more common approach which involves the elevation of written language. The linguist adduces four reasons for his stand. He points out: (i) it is part of man's biological nature that he should speak; he learns to speak unaided, but does not learn to write unless trained to do so; (ii) in all probability man in the course of evolution spoke before he began to write; (iii) everyone learns to speak before he learns to write; (iv) language changes are mainly brought about by speech.

Is the primacy of speech of any relevance to matters of language teaching especially second-language teaching? The argument that 'the speech is the language' has led H.E. Palmer and others to insist on an oral approach to the teaching of English as a second language. As Wilkins points out, "In the last three decades linguistics has provided this alternative and has thereby contributed to the re-definition of the goals that has led to the increase in the teaching of spoken language."[5]

The linguist's principal interest is in speech, but his interest is confined to the description of a language on the basis of the speech patterns he comes across in the language. He does not, however, say that the best method of teaching a language is the oral approach; nor is he qualified to express an opinion on the means by which a second language or a foreign language can be taught. All the same the fact that speech has primacy over writing has a definite pedagogic implication. That is to say, it gives the teacher the insight that the teaching of speech is as important as the teaching of writing. As David Crystal points out, "All too often the language taught is of a rather restricted kind". He adds: "It is very often a written kind of language, and not a spoken kind. In English, for example, foreigners are often taught the grammatical rules and vocabulary that are more characteristic of written English, and are given very little training in the spoken varieties. To take but one example, it is still normal for foreigners learning English to be taught to say *I shall* not *I will* and to observe the differences in meaning which it is claimed exist between the two whenever they are both used; all of which ignores the fact that the normal way of expressing future time in the verb system in speech is to use neither of them, but to say *I' ll*."[6] The practice of overemphasising "the grammatical rules and vocabulary that are more characteristic of written English" will cease when the teacher realises the importance of the spoken language. A simultaneous emphasis on written and spoken English enables the student not only to write well but also to articulate English sounds with acceptable and intelligible pronunciation and meaningful intonation and to listen to English sounds with understanding.

In our educational institutions we lay more emphasis on writing than on speaking; our text books do not generally contain exercises for oral practice. This is perhaps due to our lack of awareness of the importance of speech in the learning of a second language like English, We often tend to forget that the functions of language can best be realised only if we keep in mind that "language is used for (i) phatic communion (i.e. as a social regulator); (ii) for ceremonial purposes; (iii) as an instrument of action; (iv) to keep the records; (v) to convey orders and information; (vi) to influence people; (vii) to enable self-expression; (viii) to embody or enable thought."[7]

We do not, however, mean that speech should be the major target of English teaching in India. What is meant is that the primacy of speech should not be lost sight of while teaching English as a second language and that the sounds of English should be taught as well as the spelling and grammar of the written language. So, the teacher should have the ability to handle broad transcription besides a knowledge of the principles underlying such a transcription. Some knowledge of these principles will give the teacher an idea as to what constitutes good English speech for a second-language learner.

The study of the actual sounds of the language is called phonetics and the way in which these sounds are used, put together and organised is called phonology (or more usually phonemics in America). Phonemes are important because it is the difference in sound between them that accounts for the distinction between/t/and/ d/,/p/and/b/, etc. Accurate statements about the phonological aspects of English are made in linguistics. So, linguistics helps correct certain misconceptions about pronunciation and chart the changes in the sound system. It is here that phonetics provides the teacher with information. We cannot expect our teachers to be trained in phonetics or to have acquired phonetic skills such as those we credit a linguist with. It is, however, necessary that the teacher should have access to information on the articulatory phonetics of English. As

D.A. Wilkins observes, "The teacher who is relatively uninformed about phonetics risks transmitting quite serious errors to his pupils, especially in the earlier stages of learning..."[8] If he is well informed he knows that the rhythm of English speech is based on stress and intonation and that English is not a syllable-timed language. A teacher who is not conscious of the phonetics of English speech is likely to impart a wrong sense of the rhythm of the language to his pupils. To avoid this he should have an adequate description of natural speech available to him. This will enable him to know what is acceptable and intelligible and what is not. He should not at any rate be under the impression that pronunciation involves little more than a list of sounds. Allied to the sounds of a language is its intonation. A considerable body of descriptive material on English intonation is available, and this is useful to the teaching of English as a second language. Perhaps accurate intonation is more important than the production of accurate sounds. A word that is not clearly pronounced may be deciphered from the context in which it is used, but wrong intonation can lead to confusion and hamper communication. Intonation must therefore get more serious attention than it gets now in our schools and colleges.

According to Wilkins, phonetic transcription is "a useful tool for indicating the pronunciation of new words in class, or, more importantly in a dictionary."[9] But he also maintains that transcription on the blackboard or on paper as such without proper drilling in sounds may not be of great use in teaching pronunciation. He expresses this view because he thinks that a person who has mastered transcription can only interpret the symbols, but cannot produce them properly unless trained to do so. Wilkins also believes that diagrams of the organs of speech and detailed articulatory description will help only the potential phonetician and not the student. The important point to remember is that the practice of sounds in isolation is of limited value. Wilkins asserts: "Learning a pronunciation system is learning to operate a set of contrasts and this can only be done if the practice itself gives the pupil the opportunity to relate phonemes to one another... The most systematic approach to pronunciation teaching reflects the procedures of phonemic analysis very closely and is the product of them. It employs the technique of contrasting minimal pairs to teach pronunciation just as the linguist has used to establish inventories of phonemes. The contrastive technique is used both to ensure that the pupil does not substitute the nearest mother tongue segment for the one he is acquiring and to enable him to discriminate the phonemic contrasts of the foreign language when he hears them and to produce them when he speaks."[10]

Perhaps it is only right in this context to point out that one of the applications of linguistics in second-language teaching is to contrast the phonemes and syntax of the target language with those of the mother tongue. Every teacher knows that there is interference from the mother tongue and that this is one of the sources of errors. Linguistics helps the teacher to find out for himself what errors his pupils make and to take remedial steps to eliminate them. Here the use of mother tongue elements becomes unavoidable in second-language teaching, especially in a class in which the teacher and his pupils speak the same language. The use of the mother tongue for explaining, for instance, phonemic differences or difficult syntactical problems is sometimes frowned upon, but is effective in certain situations.

Both phonetics and phonology come to the aid of the second-language teacher; phonetics provides him with precise descriptions of the articulations whereas phonology helps him in establishing priorities of pronunciation teaching through the identification of the most important features of the sound system. A phonological level of analysis is important for the language teacher. It gives him a clear understanding of the phonetic features that the second-language learner must acquire. An inventory of phonemes or sounds will not do; for it does not take into account much significant variation in pronunciation. In short the value of a phonological description is that it indicates the targets of pronunciation teaching.

A second pedagogic implication of the linguistic approach is that it helps the teacher explain the correlation between meanings and forms in statements. The linguist's description of a language is comprehensive and it takes into account both the forms and the meanings of the language. Bloomfield in his *Language* has, however, expressed doubts about the pre-eminence given to meaning in language study.[11] This has resulted in a controversy as to the importance of meaning in the study of linguistic structures; some have even rejected meaning as an unsure basis for linguistic decisions. There is no doubt that an analysis of the syntactic functions of words is helpful for the study of a second language. But neglect of meaning and overemphasis on formal analysis may lead to uncertain conclusions such as has been pointed out by Noam Chomsky in his famous example of (i) "John is easy to please" and (ii) "John is eager to please". The structural similarity here is deceptive. The word 'eager' takes the place of 'easy' in the same pattern, but if we rewrite (i) as "It is easy to please John" and (ii) "It is eager to please John", we notice that we get a meaningful sentence in one and an absurd collocation in the other. That is to say, the meanings of 'easy' and 'eager' account for the deceptiveness of the structural similarity of the two sentences. The Bloomfieldian approach to language study has its emphasis on structural aspects and arrangements. This has reduced language learning to the mechanical acquisition of a skill in the production of certain structural devices.

Bloomfield's view is based on the theory that language is a response to some kind of stimulus and is therefore mechanistic. F.R. Morton accepts Bloomfield's view; according to him, language is a mechanical skill and learning language is developing a mechanical skill. He argues that any meaningful use of forms follows a mastery of the forms of a language and that teaching must be directed towards developing in students a skill in the use of the forms of the language. Morton's course in Spanish to Americans has been designed on the basis of the above theory.

Much present-day language teaching is allied to Morton's approach in that what is called structure drill or pattern practice lays emphasis on forms more than on meaning. Morton's approach is useful to the second-language teacher; the courses designed can be such that intensive practice of particular grammatical structures is made fully meaningful for students. It is not, however, certain whether all aspects of grammar can be taught through drilling. But some teachers claim that certain areas of grammar are best taught by means of drilling. These are concord, case, number, gender, and to some extent, word order. To the language teacher both form and meaning are important, In a sense language is conformity to certain forms, "a whole series of patterns, each type of unit having a pattern of its own and each interlocking and interacting with the other patterns at other levels."[12] The importance of linguistic structure cannot be downgraded; so too the importance of the communicative function of language cannot be rejected. In the words of D.A. Wilkins, "The soundest view is that neither should dominate but that language teaching should be based on a full understanding of both the formal and the semantic nature of language."[13] The total meaning of a sentence is the sum of its lexical meaning plus its separate meaning; the total meaning will not be clear until the grammatical structure is clear.

The linguist's study of English is data-oriented, synchronic, and descriptive. That is to say, the linguist, if he is not a historical linguist, analyses the language, and bases his analysis on available data without laying down norms about the correctness of the language. Fries's *The Structure of English* was, for example, based on recorded telephone conversations, and Randolph Quirk's *Survey of English* on readings. The point to note is that the approach of the linguist is objective and not subjective. This aspect of linguistic study is important for the teacher in so far as he too can be, like the linguist, analytical and descriptive in his approach instead of being normative and prescriptive.

Most linguists accept the distinction between the *langue* and *parole*. This is a distinction pointed out by the Swiss linguist, F. De Saussure. *Langue*, he says, is language shared by all the members of a speech community whereas parole is the act of speech of each member of the community. A similar distinction is made by Chomsky too. According to him each individual possesses competence in the use of language which is different from his performance. It is competence that the linguist describes and not performance. So too, it is *langue* that he describes and not *parole*. This is because *langue* and competence are stable whereas parole and performance are unstable, and vary from individual to individual. De Saussure says that while *parole* is not the object of study, it provides the data from which statements about *langue* can be made.

This distinction between *langue* and *parole* or competence and performance may not at first seem necessary for the teacher; moreover, insistence on *langue* may make him prescriptive in his approach. But an awareness of the distinction is helpful to him in that he will be able to ensure that he is teaching those parts of the *langue* which have the greatest practical value for his students. "What is more, instead of teaching the language in a situationally neutral context he can present it in a context which replicates as closely as possible the one for which the language is being learned. It is no longer necessary to teach the entire system. The priorities of a language course may be reversed and items of language may be included or excluded solely because the needs of the pupils, and not the overall structure of the language, have been taken as the starting point. What is learned may be smaller in quantity and greater in quality."[14]

Modern linguistics is by and large structuralist. It is structuralist because the linguist uses relational criteria; he identifies or defines linguistic categories or units on the basis of the relations between parts of a sentence. He points out that an understanding of these relations is necessary to get at the meaning of the sentence. The meaning of the individual words in a sentence will not do. The overall meaning of the sentence is likely to change if changes in the relationship of items in a sentence are effected. This structural inter-relatedness in the sentence is important for the language teacher. This is because the linguist's description of the English language is based on this inter-relatedness of the parts that constitute a sentence. In other words the linguist's description of the syntax of English gives the teacher the necessary awareness that the syntactical differences between languages count in teaching English as a second-language to the Indian student and that the syntactical dissimilarity should be brought home to him. Teaching English as a second-language in India cannot be fully effective unless the student is made aware of the syntactical difference between English and his mother-tongue. The teacher's linguistic awareness, for instance, should persuade him to make clear to the student that the structure of the sentence "A dog dug a pit" is different from that of the same sentence conveying the same meaning in his mother-tongue, say Malayalam. In Malayalam the word order will be, "A dog a pit dug". It is lack of awareness of this kind of syntactical dissimilarity that leads some Indians to say, "Where you are going?".

We have seen that linguistics is preoccupied with the phonological and structural analysis of language, that sentence is the unit which can display all the structural relations that are possible in a language, that language is a meaningful activity, and that linguistics on the whole is more occupied with the grammatical level than any other academic study connected with language. Perhaps it is because of the linguist's concentrated attention on the phonological and structural aspects of language that makes him subordinate vocabulary teaching to grammar teaching. The question, however, arises whether grammar must always dominate vocabulary. The linguist's position is that a large vocabulary by itself does not help; what is required is the ability to construct sentences. But it may be argued that the converse is also true: an ability to produce grammatical sentences is not of much value if one does not have the vocabulary, and communication becomes easy if one has a command of both vocabulary and grammar. The native speaker of English acquires vocabulary easily being exposed to the language. But this is not the case with the second-language learner. In the Indian situation in which English is taught over a period of six to eight years, it is better that both grammar and vocabulary are taught side by side. Attention, however, must be paid to the fact that words acquire their meaning not by denotation alone but also by association, collocation and connotation.

A common mistake in vocabulary teaching is to entertain the notion that for every word in the mother tongue there is an exact equivalent in the second-language. It is here that a knowledge of semantics can be of help to the teacher. D.A. Wilkins observes: "The problems of learning vocabulary are caused by the lack of equivalence between the lexical items of different languages... Vocabulary learning is learning to discriminate progressively the meanings of words in the target language from the meaning of their nearest equivalents in the mother tongue. It is also learning to make the most appropriate lexical choices for particular linguistic and situational contexts. The contribution that our understanding of vocabulary acquisition makes to teaching is largely that it enables us to define the necessary conditions for learning. The evaluation of vocabulary teaching is then a question of whether or not it meets these conditions."[15]

A certain degree of semantic awareness tells the teacher that the translation equivalent of a word from the mother-tongue does not necessarily enable the student to learn the word, though it may be helpful to understand the new word in the particular context and that translation is, therefore, unsound as a technique of teaching meaning. Learning words from graded word-lists is also unsound. Such learning tends to seek mother-tongue equivalents to these words and ignores the fact that words in their situational and linguistic isolation do not yield their full meaning. Linguistics teaches us that words should be learnt in the context of their linguistic relationship.

There are different schools of thought about language learning. Of these schools two are important; they are the behaviourist and the mentalist. The behaviourist point of view is based on the principle of stimulus, response and reinforcement. Every utterance is the result of some stimulus; the utterance forms a response to the stimulus; if the response is reinforced by acts of approval, learning takes place. The behaviourist theory is based on the assumption that language is a form of behaviour. According to Wilga M. Rivers, "Foreign language learning is basically a mechanical process of habit formation".[16] Nelson Brooks also asserts the same point of view. He says, "The single paramount fact about language learning is that it concerns, not problem solving, but the formation and performance of habits."[17] B.F. Skinner's *Verbal Behaviour* is a defence of the behaviourist theory. The mentalist theory, however, maintains that all normal living human beings are endowed with some innate internal capacity for language acquisition that other animals do not have. Noam Chomsky not only upholds this view but also vigorously refutes Skinner's assumptions about language learning.

What should be the stand of a second-language teacher in this linguistic controversy? No teacher can base his teaching of the second language entirely and exclusively on either of these theories since second- language learning is a matter of both nature and nurture. Every normal human being has the natural capacity to learn languages, but to learn a language other than the language of his environment he requires some guidance, training or nurture. In other words, learning a language requires the operation of an innate capacity—a capacity that varies from individual to individual and works most effectively when conditions are ideal. The most important condition is the aptitude of the learner. Next comes motivation; the better motivated a person is the quicker and the easier he learns the language. Age too is a factor, younger persons learn languages quicker than older persons. The right type of environment is yet another condition; of all the conditions environment is the one that can be manipulated most. Classroom atmosphere, teaching methods, aids and materials, the knowledge, preparedness, personality, persuasiveness and perseverance of the teacher, etc., constitute environment.

Every English teacher in India knows that one of the problems he has to contend with in the classroom arises from the pressure of the mother tongue on his students. That is to say, the mother tongue of the students of a particular language group learning English as a second-language influences their performance in English in such a way that almost all of them make the same mistakes in pronunciation, spelling, grammar and vocabulary. For instance, a faulty construction such as "Though he is hard-working, but he failed in the examination" in which 'but' is used instead of 'yet' or 'still' is the result of the influence of the mother tongue on the speaker. So is the utterance "I have given the examination" for "I have taken the examination".

How best can the teacher copes with this problem? Here again a little linguistic awareness on the part of the language teacher can be useful in that the branch of linguistics called contrastive linguistics helps him compare the structures of the target language and the mother tongue to determine the points where they differ. So can each phoneme in the mother tongue be compared with the phonetically most similar ones in the second language. Such contrastive descriptions and analyses can be the basis for the preparation of language texts and tests and for the correction of students learning the second language. Robert Lado's *Linguistics Across Cultures* deals with the importance of contrastive analysis in second-language teaching. He says that the inference of the student's mother tongue accounts for a number of errors and difficulties that occur at the time of learning, and afterwards in the use of the second-language. According to Lado, "...individuals tend to transfer the forms and meanings and the distribution of forms and meanings of their native language and culture to the foreign language—both productively when attempting to speak the language and act in the culture, and receptively when attempting to grasp and understand the language and the culture..."[18]

Structural differences between the target language and the mother tongue cause difficulty in learning and lead to mistakes in performance. Where structural differences are non-existent these difficulties and errors do not arise. But where differences exist, a comparative study—a contrastive analysis of—the target language and the mother tongue is necessary, as learning a second language is essentially learning to overcome difficulties and errors. Such an analysis or study will reveal the differences and make it possible for the teacher to anticipate the difficulties the learners will have and to be certain as to what he should teach. The results of the analysis can be built into language teaching materials, syllabuses, tests and research for the benefit of teachers and students.

What we have said above does not mean that the second-language teacher should be a linguist. Linguistics and language teaching are two different activities. There is, however, much in linguistics that can be of use in language teaching. This does not mean that the findings of the linguist should be wholly accepted by the teacher. Language teaching is a pragmatic business and no teacher should rely solely on the data drawn from linguistics; good linguistics may turn out to be bad psychology and ineffective pedagogy. Classroom techniques can hardly be guided by linguistics.

But there is a relation between linguistics and language teaching; this cannot be ignored. Linguistics increases one's awareness and understanding of the nature of language. Perhaps it does not give us specific points of information that can be built into our language teaching programme. It, however, enables us to define the goals of learning, determine the broad methodological approach, assess the value of particular techniques, and organise the language content. In short, as David Crystal points out, linguistics enables the teacher to 'know about' the language he is called upon to teach rather than merely 'know' it. According to him, "Language teaching is probably the most widespread application linguistics has these days..."[19] What the language teacher stands to gain by his knowledge of linguistics can best be summed up in the words of D.A. Wilkins: "The real contribution of linguistics is to increase one's understanding of the nature of language. Anyone who has studied linguistics is sensitized to language and thereby to the complexity of language learning. (He) will be better able to exercise critical judgment of attractive innovations in language teaching, including those that may claim to be supported by linguistic research. Language teaching still depends very heavily on the intuitive interpretation that the teacher constantly has to make—interpretations of learning and of language. The study of linguistics roots those intuitions in a more complete understanding of language and in doing so refines them. This is why, in my judgment, the insights provided by linguistics, however, insubstantial they may appear, may ultimately be more significant than the 'new facts' it offers. There may be no operational definition of grammatical complexity and simplicity, but through his knowledge of the type of structure that language has, the linguistically sophisticated teacher's judgment is better informed, though still subjective. The idea of teaching the most suitable vocabulary for a given group of learners may be just as effective in correcting bad vocabulary content as the rigorous application of a set of selectional criteria. The awareness that appropriateness of language choice is also a stylistic matter and that error is not to be identified solely with grammar, vocabulary or spelling, will prove as valuable to the teacher as any actual description of stylistic features that is yet available... The value of linguistics is that by increasing his awareness of language, it makes him more competent and therefore a better language teacher."[20]

References

1. Allen, Haroid B., (Ed.), *Teaching English as a Second Language,* p. 74. The quotation is from "Applied Linguistics in the Classroom" by William G. Moulton.
2. ibid., p. 74
3. Wilkins, D. A., *Linguistics in Language Teaching,* London: Edward Arnold, 1980, p. 23
4. Fries, Charles C., *Linguistics: the Study of Language,* New York: Rinehart and Winston Inc., 1964, pp. 91-92
5. ibid., p. 9
6. Crystal, David, *Linguistics,* Hammondsworth: Penguin Books, 1971, p. 22
7. Wallwork, J.F., *Language and Linguistics,* London: Heinemann Educational Books, 1971, p. 12
8. ibid., p. 39
9. ibid., p. 56
10. ibid., p. 57
11. Bloomfield, L., *Language,* London: Allen and Unwin, 1935, p. 140
12. Wallwork, J.F., op.cit., p. 62
13. Wilkins, D.A., op.cit., p. 24
14. ibid., p. 36
15. ibid., p. 130
16. Rivers, Wilga M., *The Psychologist and the Foreign Language Teacher,* Chicago: University of Chicago Press, 1964, p. 31
17. Brooks, Nelson, *Language and Language Learning,* New York: Harcourt, Brace & World, 1960, pp. 46-47

18.   Lado, Robert, *Linguistics Across Cultures,* Ann Arbor: University of Michigan Press, 1957, p.2

19.   Crystal, David, op. cit., p. 25

20.   Wilkins, D.A., op. cit., p. 229

For Further Reading

1.   Wilkins, D.A., *Linguistics in Language Teaching,* London: Edward Arnold, 1980

2.   Fries, Charles C., *Linguistics: the Study of Language,* New York: Holt, Rinehart & Winston Inc., 1964

3.   Crystal, David, *Linguistics,* Hammondsworth: Penguin Book, 1971

4.   Wallwork, J.F., *Language and Linguistics,* London: Heinemann Educational Books, 1971

5.   Lado, Robert, *Linguistics Across Cultures,* Ann Arbor: University of Michigan Press, 1957

FIVE

TEACHING ENGLISH GRAMMAR

Every language has its grammar. Whether it is one's own mother tongue or a second-language that one is learning, the grammar of the language is important. This is because acceptability and intelligibility, both in speech and in writing within as well as outside one's own circle or group, depend on the currently followed basic notions and norms of grammaticality. A knowledge of grammar is perhaps more important to a second-language learner than to a native speaker. This is because in the process of acquiring the language the native speaker has intuitively internalised the grammar of the language whereas the second-language learner has to make a conscious effort to master those aspects of the language which account for grammaticality. It is, therefore, necessary for us, to whom English is a second-language, to learn the grammar of the language.

In order that we may decide for ourselves our approach to the study of grammar, we should know what 'grammar' means to us. This is important in view of the fact that the place of English grammar in the school and college curriculum, the methods of teaching it, and its purpose and value have been the subject of controversy in recent years.

The term 'grammar' has meant various things at various times and often several things at the same time. English grammar in the beginning was greatly influenced by Latin grammar. Because of this influence the term 'grammar' was used at first to refer to all language study. Later, it came to denote linguistic etiquette: the right and the wrong way to use English. In the eighteenth century Joseph Priestley, a many-sided scholar and scientist, made a feeble effort to warn against importing too much of Latin grammar into English grammar. He said, "Language is a method of conveying our ideas to the minds of other persons, and the grammar of any language is a collection of observations on the structure of it, and a system of rules for the proper use of it."[1]

The school grammars that were published subsequently, for example, C.T. Onion's and J.C. Nesfield's, followed the same tradition as the one started by Priestley; these grammars, however, were authoritative and were expected to provide unequivocal answers in the same way as a dictionary provides meanings. In recent years the grammars of the Nesfield school have been heavily criticized as normative or prescriptive. Today what is followed is a 'linguistic approach'; the merit of this approach is that it is descriptive. But here too we find differences among the grammarians; these differences are basically owing to their being structural, behaviouristic or pragmatic in their approach. Since they belong to different linguistic schools, they propose different models with differing theoretical implications. Each school has its own definition of 'grammar' backed by a multitude of abstractions. For example, to some the word 'grammar' refers to inflexions, forms, paradigms, conjugations, etc., whereas to Chomsky it means "simply a system of rules that in some explicit and well-defined way assigns structural descriptions to sentences."[2]

In the first chapter of his book, *Writing Transformational Grammars: an Introduction*[3], Andreas Koutsoudas gives us a definition of 'grammar' after Chomsky. He says: "A grammar is a device that generates (i.e. enumerates) an infinite number of correct sentences of a given language and no incorrect ones." He explains further that "a grammar is a device that tells the reader how to construct an infinite number of correct sentences of a language, and no incorrect ones". According to Koutsoudas the word 'device' can be replaced by 'finite set of rules', 'correct sentences' by 'grammatical or well-formed sentences', and 'incorrect sentences' by 'ungrammatical sentences'. With these substitutions he rewrites the definition thus: "A grammar is a finite set of rules which generates an infinite number of grammatical sentences of a given language and no ungrammatical ones." The definition implies that only those sentences of which there is the least doubt as to their grammaticality are grammatical sentences; this is an important point because in any language there are sentences whose grammaticality is questionable. Another point to note is that while a grammar generates an infinite number of sentences, the set of rules that generates them is finite.

The definitions of 'grammar' lead us to the fact that grammar consists of certain rules and that it is these rules that govern the system of language units and structures by which we communicate with each other. That is to say, the study of grammar can help us in communication as grammar is a system consisting of phonology (language sounds—the vowels and the consonants represented by the alphabet), morphology (word form-the differences between 'beauty', 'beautiful', 'beautifully' and 'beautify'), semantics (meaning and meaning relationship in language), and syntax (word relationships and word order or sequence). The grammar of a language is thus essentially a logical, complete explanation of the way language operates. The complete grammar of any language would then be a guide in detail to the processes we go through in making sentences even though we are unconscious of them as we speak and write our hundreds of sentences every day.

What is important to note is that internalising the rules of grammar is necessary for us to communicate in a language. But the question remains: what should be our approach to the study of grammar? Over the years three approaches have been followed in the study of English grammar. These approaches which have had and are having a great deal of influence upon our attitudes towards grammar are the traditional, the structural and the transformational-generative.

Before the eighteenth century the study of the English language was neglected. Many Englishmen could not read and write and the few who could, preferred the classical languages (Greek and Latin) to English for their written documents; this is because these languages were the traditional languages of scholarship—the means by which the wisdom of the ancients had been passed down. Latin, in particular, was the language of the Church and the University, and was used widely by the educated throughout Europe. By the eighteenth century, however, the knowledge of the Renaissance had been translated into the language everybody spoke. This and the gradual use of English for affairs of State and literature and the invention of the printing press generated a need for the study of grammar. Characteristic of the age itself was a strong desire for regulation and order—observable in philosophy, literature, architecture and scientific thought. It was natural, then, that scholars should want to codify what they felt was a disorderly language. And when various academies and committees failed to 'improve and correct' English, individual scholars took on the task.

These scholars believed in universal grammar—a perfect grammar of which individual grammars were corruptions. (This belief in a universal grammar exists even today; this is because some grammatical features are shared by all languages.) Because the educated Englishmen of the eighteenth century knew Latin so well that they naturally believed that this classical language must be the closest to the universal grammar. The differences between English and Latin they considered errors or corruptions of English. The grammar textbooks of the period, then, were written to correct these errors and to prescribe desirable usage. As Dr. Johnson said in the Preface to his dictionary, "I have laboured to refine our language to grammatical purity, and to clear it from colloquial barbarism, licentious idioms, and irregular combinations."

In order to establish a language as 'perfect' as human beings could create, early grammarians obviously had to use Latin as a model from which to build an English grammar. Their difficulties were great, however, for as we know today, Latin and English differ significantly from one another despite their Indo-European ancestry.

In Latin, morphology (word form) is far more important than syntax (word order). In English, however, we rely more on syntax than we do on morphology. It is true that we alter word form in English too; 'run' is changed into 'ran' or 'drive' into 'drives'. But we can understand an English sentence in which the usual form changes are not made; for example, there is no difficulty in understanding the sentence, "The engine of the car run well when he drive the car fast". The intended meaning of the sentence will not be grasped by us if our understanding depends primarily upon word form. As it is, however, it makes sense though it sounds awkward.

What is essential to our understanding of English is syntax or word order. The sentence "Engine well runs the fast car the of drives the car he fast when" is unintelligible because its order is simply not common to the English language system. In Latin nearly the opposite is true. The form of most Latin words is more important than their position. Generally, failure to alter the form of Latin words results in confusion. But except for a few like *ad* and *cum*, most Latin words do not have fixed places within a sentence.

To handle the discrepancies between the two languages, eighteenth century grammarians established many rules. And though these rules may have originally been derived from the operations of Latin grammar, they soon came to express the arbitrary judgment of textbook authors—when to use *shall* instead of *will*, for instance. These rules prescribed behaviour in the use of English. Those who followed them were 'right' and those who did not were 'wrong'. There was no 'betwixt and between'.

More problems appeared when the grammarians attempted to analyse English structures in two ways some in terms of lexical (dictionary) meaning and others in terms of grammatical function.

Probably the most widely known definition of the sentence is based upon meaning: "A sentence is a group of words expressing a complete thought". But what exactly is a thought? And if we could define it, how would we determine its completeness?

Another popular definition is functional: "A sentence must have a subject which names a person, place, thing or idea, and a predicate which says something about the subject". This explains a construction like "The child is crying". But couldn't "the crying child" also fit the definition? The word 'child' names a person, and the word 'crying' says something about the child.

The definitions of parts of speech are inconsistent. Some are explained in terms of meaning (e.g., "a noun names a person, place or thing"); others are explained in terms of function (e.g. "a conjunction connects words, phrases or sentences").

Despite inconsistencies like these the English grammar that was codified in the eighteenth century still exists with very little change in what is known as traditional grammar with its "correctness rules". Not all these rules and concepts were bad ones, but some of them caused a great number of misunderstandings about the nature of English; also, they have caused many of us to become frustrated and inhibited in the use of English. Many linguists were, therefore, highly critical of the traditional grammar and even attempted to discredit practically all of this grammar.

Today we have a set of linguists who look at language in a way different from that of the traditional grammarians. Their goals, however, are similar to those of the traditionalists: (i) to increase man's knowledge about his language; (ii) to make that knowledge accurate and truthful. But their methods are radically different. Instead of making judgments about how English should be used, modern linguists describe and analyse the elements of language, using inductive methods similar to those followed in Chemistry, Physics and other sciences. In other words, they do not prescribe language use, but describe it. Consequently, their work has come to be known as descriptive linguistics.

What is the reason for this change in emphasis? Essentially linguists consider the entire framework of traditional grammar invalid. Influenced by the scientific orientation of the twentieth century, they believe that the raw data of language, namely speech, should be studied and described in order to build a sufficient body of facts from which useful generalizations might be made. In doing this they emphasise the concept that language is speech rather than writing and thus give a new orientation towards the concept of usage. In applying the truths these linguists have learnt about language to the teaching of English grammar in our schools and colleges, they have evolved certain procedures used currently in what is known as structural grammar.

One of the primary characteristics of structural grammar is its division of the study of the language into two basic parts: structure and meaning. In general, the structural grammarian prefers to study the grammatical forms or structures of the language before considering lexical meanings. He feels that the opposite approach, used by the traditional grammarian, interferes in the discovery of precisely how language works—that it keeps us from seeing that English is a system learnt by a recognition of certain repeated grammatical signals.

Considering English grammar in terms of structure is not so complicated as it seems. The native speakers remember learning lexical meanings because this takes place every time they encounter a new word. They do not learn grammatical signals because this happens early and informally in their lives. But the second-language learner is not in the same position as the native speaker. He does not become as naturally exposed to the language as the native speaker. His internalisation of grammatical structures, though not complicated, is through deliberate exposure to the language. So, he has to learn both lexical meanings and grammatical signals more or less at the same time.

To examine structure, the linguist begins with the sounds peculiar to English. He then records the sounds with the help of a set of symbols which are based on the phonetic alphabet and which are designed particularly for that purpose. In this procedure words are represented as follows: 'write' /rait/; 'cute' /kju:t/: 'ready-made' /redi'meid/. The smallest sound units which can be recorded (vowels and consonants, for example) are called phonemes, and they group together to form meaningful units of sound called morphemes. Semantically meaningful units of sound which appear alone in English are called free morphemes (e.g. 'boy', 'table', 'walk', etc.) and those which do not appear alone are called bound morphemes (e.g. '-er'; '-est', '-s'). A word like 'reader' is a combination of a free morpheme ('read') and a bound morpheme ('-er').

How do sounds become grammatically meaningful? The answer in brief is that they gain identity by (i) intonation, (ii) word form, and (iii) word order or sequence. If we regard the human voice as a kind of musical instrument through which we make sounds by breathing out and by manipulating the tongue, the lips, and so forth, then the meaning of intonation becomes apparent. Intonation involves pitch (the raising or lowering of voice level), stress (the emphasis upon a sound) and juncture (the interruption of the flow of sound)—all qualities which produce what we commonly call one's tone of voice. Each of the three elements of intonation acts to group sounds into grammatical units.

By studying word form and word order as well as intonation, linguists have redefined the traditional parts of speech, classifying them solely upon the basis of structure, and designating these classes form classes.

Nouns, for instance, take certain endings and appear repeatedly in specific positions in sentences. This is also true of verbs, adverbs and adjectives. Other words, called function words, serve to group these four major classes (and certain pronouns which are a subclass of nouns) into sentence patterns basic to the English language.

To analyse the grammatical properties of English sentences according to structure, we use the signals of intonation, word form and word order while at the same time we ignore the lexical meaning of individual words. Linguists frequently demonstrate this principle by analysing sentences utterly devoid of lexical meaning such as the following:

The bosy raths minsly bonged the torps.

From previous observations the structural grammarian knows that most English sentences consist of nouns followed by verbs, that these nouns are frequently signalled by special words like 'a', 'an', and 'the' which are known as function words, and that nouns, verbs, adjectives and adverbs may be distinguished by characteristic endings. Using this information he can tell us the form class of each word in the sentence and how it functions:

FW	ADJ	N	ADV	V	FW	N
The	bosy	raths	minsly	bonged	the	torps

Furthermore, the structural grammarian will point out that although we are not linguists, most of us can probably identify the elements in the sentences—without being able to define their meanings.

This much information on English grammatical concepts, limited as it is, confirms that a 'no-nonsense' example, "The child is crying", is a sentence. But it does not really tell us whether or not "the crying child" is a sentence. Experts have observed, however, that some utterances stand alone, while others always occur with another utterance. For example, we do not use "as soon as", "in the morning", or "when he spoke" as separate utterances, but as parts of other expressions or as responses to other utterances: "I will write this paper as soon as I can"; "When are you going?", "In the morning"; "When he spoke I knew him"; "When did you recognise him?", "When he spoke".

Many structural grammarians then would regard a sentence to be an utterance which may occur alone or one which may occur in response to a previous construction. To distinguish between the utterances mentioned, the first type is sometimes referred to as a major sentence and the second type as a minor sentence. Major sentences appear alone; minor sentences (identified usually as phrases or clauses in written English) do not appear alone. In addition, certain definite arrangements of grammatical elements recur with major sentences. In fact they recur so obviously and so often that they are known as the basic sentence patterns of the English language.

In addition to grammatical distinctions like these, the structural grammarian notes that numerous constructions seem to consist of two parts, parts he designates immediate constituents. The immediate constituents are customarily the subject and the predicate. To illustrate this, the structural grammarian may use one of a number of diagram-like methods, some of which are very different from the diagrams used in traditional grammar. A main distinction, however, is that the structural grammarian does not change the word order primarily because it is the relationship between words (syntax) which is most important to him. All this becomes clear if we analyse an example:

The thin boy with shaggy hair could answer difficult questions. The structural grammarian might ask us first to mark pairs of words which we feel have the closest relationships. Our diagram might then look like this:

The *thin boy* with *shaggy hair could answer difficult questions.* Our next step would be to group these pairs of words according to clear relationships. Certainly we cannot group 'shaggy hair' and 'could answer'; therefore, our grouping must be like this:

The *thin boy with shaggy hair could answer difficult questions.* There is a definite break between 'hair' and 'could', but the group 'the thin boy with shaggy hair' (the subject) does have a definite relationship to the second group 'could answer difficult questions' (the predicate).

Whatever be its merits, immediate constituent analysis has some weaknesses. One of the weaknesses is that the point of division is not always clear and that it may vary slightly depending upon the structural grammarian. Another weakness consists in the fact that some word groups simply do not lend themselves to immediate constituent analysis.

What is of great significance to us, however, is that structural grammarians work with structures in use and do not seek the help of another language system. Furthermore, they have established that the recurring forms and sequences of English comprise a signalling system which is instrumental to our communicative ability.

Structural grammar has been an innovative and important approach to the discovery of knowledge about English. Consequently, it has been called new grammar. All the same many linguists feel today that structural grammar does not sufficiently explain the operations of the English language. It provides an analysis for a given sample of language, and serves as a practical approach to the study of the language in the classroom, but it does not reveal how English sentences are produced in the first place. To determine this and to establish still newer truths about the English language, a number of scholars have developed what is known as transformational-generative grammar.

While the traditionalists seek to prescribe language use and the structuralists attempt to describe it, the transformational-generative grammarians want to theorise it by discovering an explanation that will solve the remaining mysteries of grammar.

The most provocative of these mysteries is the competence of the native speaker of English. How does a native speaker manage to compose grammatical sentences which he has never heard before? Conversely, how is he able to utter sentences which are unique? At the same time how does he comprehend differences in sentences which appear to be the same in structure, yet are different in meaning as in 'John is easy to please' and 'John is eager to please'?

Noam Chomsky's book, *Syntactic Structures,* published in 1957, was the first significant attempt by a linguist to account for this aspect of language. According to Chomsky the structural approach, based on an examination of a given number of utterances, though valuable, is limited for at least three reasons: (i) it deals with a comparatively small sampling of language which is subject to change; (ii) it describes the state of this language sample, but not the operations of a language as a whole; (iii) it describes the performance (i.e. the sentences we may produce at a given time), but not competence (i.e. the knowledge we have of how to produce sentences).

Chomsky maintains that competence in the use of language comes from an innate knowledge of certain rules or principles which govern the operations of language. These rules are not the directives we come across in traditional grammar which say what is right and what is wrong. But they represent certain systematic processes which occur in language. Since our knowledge is internal and cannot be described, grammarians find it necessary to hypothesize a representation of it.

The meaning of grammar then assumes still another dimension in the work of the transformationalists. When they speak of grammar, they are not speaking of description itself, but of the particular theory which according to them, provides a complete, consistent explanation of the way a language operates. The difference between a linguistic theory and a linguistic description is that the latter describes a body of historically given utterances whereas the former not only describes the same body of historically given utterances but also describes possible future utterances. The theory explains and describes what is in existence and also predicts what will be.

The transformational-generative approach to language is characterised by abstraction. This is more so because of the transformationalist's use of modern symbolic logic (what appears to be a long series of algebra like equations) and a great deal of new terminology to present the theories. It is here that the transformational-generative grammar becomes most complex and most annoying to its critics. In spite of the difficulty experienced by ordinary people in understanding the transformational concepts, yet they may well become the most important ones regarding language.

The transformationalists' emphasis is upon the sentence. They point out that when we learn a language we do not learn individual words or sentences out of context; instead we learn a mechanism or device which enables us to compose sentences.

We might regard our sentence-producing mechanism as a computer. Items go into the computer and sentences come out of it. Roughly speaking, these items are: (i) the sounds we pronounce in sentences, (ii) the structures which compose sentences, and (iii) the meanings we hope to convey in sentences. The sentences produced by our internal computer are first of all grammatical ones and are produced with the help of sets of rules. In other words, the components of a transformational-generative grammar are: its (i) phonological component, (ii) syntactic component, and (iii) semantic component. The exact relationship of these aspects is still unknown. But linguists are hard at work on it. In contrast to the structuralists' emphasis upon phonology, transformationalists have given the syntactic component the most attention. One of the significant discoveries is that syntax has two principles or sets of rules which underlie the formation of sentences. These are: (i) phrase-structure rules and (ii) transformational rules.

Phrase-structure rules relate to the 'generative' aspect of transformational-generative grammar. The generative grammar contains (i) lists or 'sets' of symbols, and (ii) rules which tell us how to combine the symbols so that we might create all the sentences of a language—if this were possible. Transformationalists, like structuralists, recognise that there are sentences basic to the language—sentences from which all others are derived. These simple declarative sentences produced by phrase-structure rules they call *kernels*, and the many sentences which are variations upon these basic ones they designate *transformations*.

Instead of breaking an existing sentence down to its immediate constituents the transformationalist attempts to create the original formation of the sentence. A basic *kernel* sentence is represented in symbols by the following phrase-structure rule:

$$S \longrightarrow NP + VP$$

The symbols are simply an economical way of stating that sentence (S) consists of a noun phrase (NP) and a verb phrase (VP) in that order. The arrow means 'must be rewritten as'. Sometimes the same rule is expressed graphically by what is called a branching tree diagram.

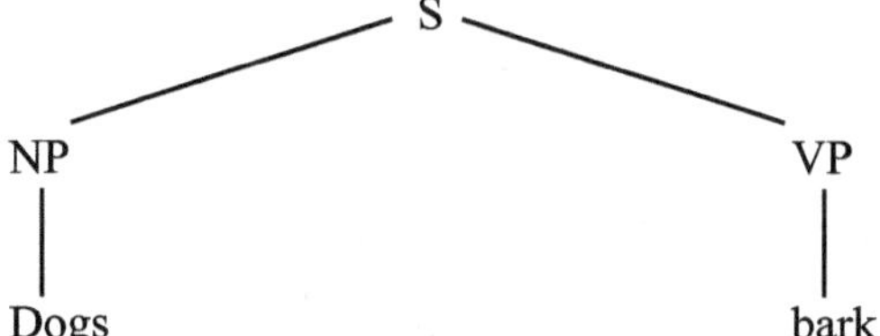

The transformationalist, like the structuralist, makes clear that a basic sentence is made up of a subject (NP) and a predicate (VP).

Additional phrase-structure rules specify the kinds of NP's and VP's which comprise kernel sentences. In transformational-generative grammar NP may mean either a single word or a group of words—either a noun alone, as in the above example, a noun preceded by 'the' or 'his' or a noun substitute like 'she' or 'they'. Similarly, VP may mean either a single verb plus its object or a verb plus an adverb. Sentences like 'The dogs bark loudly', 'The boy hit the ball', etc., are typical kernel sentences generated by phrase-structure rules.

The children of native speakers learn somehow to make all these kernel sentences. The phrase-structure rules then are a representation of how the transformationalist thinks our internal sentence-making mechanism works. Even at an early age, however, these children begin to make more complicated sentences than these basic ones. These sophisticated sentences, derived from the kernels, are made by means of transformational rules. The children are not aware that they apply these rules, but it is the rules that make it possible for them to (i) rearrange the elements of the kernel, (ii) expand elements of the kernel, or (iii) delete elements from the kernel.

Probably the easiest transformation to understand is the interrogative. In this instance the rule shows us how to arrange elements so that from a kernel like 'John is going home' we can derive the question 'Is John going home?'. Another rule transforms 'I heard the news' and 'John's team won' into 'I heard the news that John's team won'. Still another rule serves to delete while transforming 'She was baking a cake' into 'She was baking'.

These transformations are simple ones, but the entire process becomes increasingly complicated as more transformational operations are needed to account for sentences which contain clauses, phrases, or passive voice, for example. All the transformational rules, like the phrase-structure rules, appear in symbols with arrows separating the structure as it is, and the structure as it may be rewritten. So, while we take our sentence-making ability for granted, producing long sentences with ease, the transformationalist's representation is itself a considerable achievement—sometimes requiring pages of mathematical notations (which boggle the mind of the ordinary student).

In addition to outlining the operations which characterise sentence-making, transformationalists are seeking an explanation of our ability to recognise the difference in meaning between sentences like 'John is eager to please' and 'John is easy to please'. Transformationalists suggest that in addition to syntactic rules there are rules of phonology which serve to convert the abstraction of every sentence into its pronounceable form, and rules of semantics which generate interpretations of sentences. Though much work is still to be done, transformational-generative grammar to this extent suggests the kind of relationship which exists between these major aspects of language.

Whether the transformational-generative approach to grammar is a natural outgrowth of structural grammar or an entirely separate theory is difficult to say, since not all linguists agree on this point. Those who consider it a development of earlier work generally believe that it refines sentence analysis beyond the point reached by structural study. Those who consider it a separate theory believe that the two approaches—structural and transformational—generative—cannot be reconciled.

Whether transformational-generative grammar is related to traditional grammar is a somewhat easier question since most linguists seem to agree that it is. The main resemblance is found in the notion of a universal grammar-the idea that general principles exist which govern the operations of language and which are applicable to all languages. A corollary is that these principles relate in some way to the intrinsic properties of the mind.

In spite of the disagreement which exists between linguists regarding the relationship of traditional, structural, and transformational-generative grammar, some predict an eventual synthesis of all these approaches to the study of language. Each approach has made a valuable contribution to our knowledge of English, and each has assimilated some of the facts and methods of the one preceding it.

From the foregoing summary of the three main approaches to grammar one thing is quite evident: the study of grammar is an integral part of the study of language; we cannot, however, teach grammar dissociating it from the language. It is also clear that the knowledge of grammar enables us to use the language in an acceptable and intelligible manner. Both descriptive and prescriptive approaches aim at improving the language learner's receptive and productive skills.

The prescriptive grammarians try to lay down what sort of language ought to be used whereas the descriptive grammarians are more concerned with trying to describe what language is used. The approach of the descriptive grammarian leads us to the notion that more than one form may be acceptable and that correctness is a matter of conforming to the language fashions around us. In the prescriptive, traditional approach certain usages are condemned as incorrect. For example, we have the use of 'It's me' instead of 'It's I' or 'He is taller than me' instead of 'He is taller than I'. The conventional notion of correctness insisted upon by prescriptive grammarians is the result of the influence of Latin grammar on English grammar and has perhaps lost its validity since English unlike Latin is a living language and good English is not always 'correct' English. As Quirk says: "Most of the 'problems' of English grammar crop up because of a clash between the very definite but often very different conventions of the wider circle of the nation as a whole."[4] But as teachers and learners of English as a second-language our effort should be to learn what may be called Standard English as defined by Quirk himself in *The Use of English*.. One of the points Quirk emphasises is that "so far as the majority of the grammatical features are concerned, there is no disagreement among the members of the English-speaking world about what is right and what is wrong."[5] Our approach to the teaching of grammar should be such that we should draw the attention of our students to the general patterns of the language as it is spoken and written by the educated English-speaking community without laying down what sort of language ought to be used. To quote Quirk once again: "The very fact that usage is divided, that we are all aware that some say one thing and some another in these disputed areas, should itself make it obvious that it is impossible to call one 'correct' and the other 'incorrect'. One might as well argue about whether 'begin to work' is more correct than 'start to work' or whether a plain tie is more correct than a striped one, cotton underwear more correct than nylon."[6]

In India too as in the West there is a lot of discussion on the teaching of English grammar and correctness. Certain articles and letters published in The Hindu in May-June 1982 reflect the nature of the debate. When Anniah Gowda, D. Anjaneyulu and N. Chandrasekharan are for the teaching of grammar along traditional lines, S. Swaminathan and S. Vishnu Bhat are for the direct method of teaching. Gowda says: "We should go back to the study of grammar. The dry-as-dust English teaching, harnessed to the demands of grammar and syntax, what Sydney Smith called 'the nonsense of grammar' has to be re-adopted. What we need to restore is the teaching of correct English as the essential craft through which all writing whether creative or not must be expressed. Children do need to learn the basic rules of grammar as well as what is regarded as good practice. If they do not, they will neither be able to express 'accurately' what they mean nor learn to discriminate when reading or listening to what other people have to say."[7]

In their plea for the direct method of teaching, Swaminathan and Bhat say: "It is well to remember that the object of English teaching in India is not to produce a Winston Churchill or a J. Krishnamurthi, but to equip generations of young men and women to transact their professional life which is predominantly English speaking. The direct method of teaching (the approach which is sometimes unscientifically called the functional approach) would seem more useful than the pedantic and pedagogic grammar-patronising approach."[8]

Many and serious confusions and conflicts seem to be there all over the world in the field of grammar teaching. Yet teaching grammar seems to find favour with teachers, examiners, and educational theorists, each for his own reason. The teacher finds it less difficult to teach grammar; to the examiner grammar questions are easy to set and correct; the educational theorist believes that grammar gives a training in reasoning. The main argument in favour of teaching grammar is that it is a good discipline and that it has intellectual appeal, apart from practical benefits.

There are also arguments put forward against the teaching of grammar. P.Gurrey in his book Teaching English Grammar (London: Longman, 1961) sums up these arguments thus: (i) what is learnt in a grammar class is not applied with sufficient point and frequency; grammatical rules may be thoroughly understood and learnt by a student and yet not applied in practice; (ii) most of the definitions of grammatical forms and functions are not satisfactory; (iii) the traditional method of teaching grammar with its emphasis on parsing of words, word relationships, grammatical functions and analysis is inadequate.

Michael West who is an advocate of the principle of controlled vocabulary believes that "the cure for bad grammar is not more grammar but short advances within a graded and controlled vocabulary followed by long plateaus of assimilation". He, however, lists the following points in favour of teaching grammar: (i) grammar teaches us "the concealed liabilities of a vocabulary"; (ii) grammar is a set of labour-saving rules, explanations and patterns which economise effort in language learning; (iii) grammar is a preventive and corrective medicine, safeguarding or rectifying those points which are especially liable to error.[9]

In this confusion of differing approaches, theories, debates and discussions on the usefulness or otherwise of the teaching of grammar what should be the standpoint of a teacher of English in India? Certainly he cannot do without grammar. Grammar is essential to second-language learning. As Wilkins observes: "The acquisition of the grammatical system of a language remains a most important element in language learning. The grammar is the means through which linguistic creativity is ultimately achieved and an inadequate knowledge of the grammar would lead to serious limitations on the creativity for communication. A notional syllabus, no less than a grammatical syllabus, must seek to ensure that the grammatical system is properly assimilated by the learner."[10] What Wilkins means is that grammar should be taught; without a knowledge of the grammar of the language, one's learning of the language is inadequate; conscious learning of grammar is slowly converted into an automatic process.

Once it is admitted that teaching grammar is necessary the question arises: how is it to be taught? We have seen that the insights of modern linguistics have given us the structural approach and the transformational-generative approach in preference to the traditional approach. There is much to be said in favour of the descriptive approach. But prescriptivism inherent in the traditional approach, though reprehensible from a purely linguistic point of view, can be a help to the teacher, for his task is to lead his students to a certain degree of conformity through the laying down of norms. A good teacher should, therefore, be eclectic in his approach; he need not accept any one theory in toto; he should select what is best suited for his purpose in the classroom. He need not have a whole-hearted commitment to traditional grammar, nor should he reject outright the insights of modern linguistics. He should explain and describe the grammatical aspects of structures, illustrate them with examples and lay down certain rules for his students' guidance and practice. In other words he should have his own approach based on a synthesis of the insight he has acquired from his study of the different approaches to the teaching of grammar.

References

1.   Quoted on p. 216 in *English Grammar* (London: Heinemann Educational Books, 1969) by F.S. Scott and others
2.   Chomsky, Noam, *Aspects of the Theory of Syntax,* Massachusetts: MIT Press, 1965, p.1
3.   Koutsoudas, Andreas, *Writing Transformational Grammars: an Introduction,* New York: McGraw-Hill Book Company, 1966, p.2
4.   Quirk, Randolph, *The Use of English*, p. 110
5.   ibid., p. 110
6.   ibid., p. 114
7.   *The Hindu, May* 11, 1982
8.   *The Hindu, June* 10, 1982.
9.   West, Michael, "How much English Grammar?", *ELT Selections* 1, 1952, p. 30
10. Wilkins, David, *Notional Syllabuses,* Oxford University Press, 1976, p.3

For Further Reading

1.   Allen, J.P.B. and Corder, S.P., *The Edinburgh Course in Applied Linguistics,* Vol. 3, London: Oxford University Press, 1974
2.   Gurrey, P., *Teaching English Grammar,* London: Longman, 1961
3.   Krashen, S.D., *Second Language Acquisition and Second Language Learning,* Oxford: Pergamon Press, 1981
4.   —, *Principles and Practice in Second Language Acquisition,* Oxford: Pergamon Press, 1982
5.   Morris, L., *The Art of Teaching English as a Second Language,* London: Macmillan, 1985
6.   Palmer, Frank, *Grammar,* (Penguins), The English Language Book Society, 1978
7.   Thomson, A.J. and Martinet, A.V., *A Practical English Grammar,* London: Oxford University Press, 1969
8.   Widdowson Henny G., *Teaching Language as Communication* London: Oxford University Press, 1979

SIX

METHODS AND PRINCIPLES

Over the years there have been different methods employed for the teaching of English as a second-language. These methods may be mentioned here. The earliest method is the one generally known as the Grammar-Translation Method. This is actually the same as the method used for teaching classical languages like Latin and Greek and is also called the 'Classical Method'. The method insisted on the memorisation of grammatical rules and translation of related texts, and paid little attention to speaking and reading as skills to be developed. The method presupposes that the process of translation will enable the student to master the syntax, phraseology, idioms etc., of the second-language. According to H.E. Palmer, this method is replete with weaknesses. He catalogues these weaknesses as follows: "It is one which treats all languages as if they were dead, as if each consisted essentially of a collection of ancient documents to be deciphered and analysed... It is the one which categorically ignores all considerations of phonetics, pronunciation and acoustic image, and boldly places language on a foundation of alphabets, spellings and writing systems... It is the one which assumes translation to be the main or only procedure for the learning of vocabulary ... It is the one which assumes that word and sentence structure is to be attained mainly or solely through the memorising of the so-called rules of grammar."[1]

As a reaction against the Grammar-Translation Method, there came into vogue the Natural Method. This was based on the belief that the best one could do to teach a foreign language was 'to follow nature'. That is to say, the maximum exposure of the child to the target language without the least interference from the mother tongue, would enable the child to learn the language.

The Natural Method in course of time was reformed, and this gave rise to what is commonly known as the Direct Method. The Direct Method is a logical extension of the Natural Method; it is also an offshoot of the Behaviourist School of Psychology. It insists that the key to all language learning lies in association; it stresses the need for direct association between experience and expression in the foreign language. The aim is to enable the student to think in the foreign language and to cultivate an unerring language sense. This method recognises that language sense has its roots in the spoken language and lays stress on the Oral Approach.

The Direct Method has certain limitations. For one thing the method is not all that direct; for only a limited number of words can be directly associated with their meanings or the objects they represent. Moreover, its main claim that it teaches a foreign language directly, and not through the mother tongue, is only partly true. As D.H. Stott says, "The clever youngster thrives on the Direct Method by defeating it."[2] The mother tongue equivalents of words may not be used by the teacher but may be in the student's mind, and the student does not exclude them from his own mind.

Another limitation of this method arises from its neglect of the language skills like writing and reading because of overemphasis on oral work. The Direct Method practically ignores the study of grammar; this is not desirable because a knowledge of grammar is useful to the students to correct errors and strengthen language habits.

In spite of these limitations it may be admitted that the Natural Method and the Direct Method are historically important. This is because these two methods stress the primacy of speech and habit-formation through repetition in language learning and enable the students to have a real command of the target language and have thus considerable influence on modern language pedagogy.

The main problem in teaching a second-language lies in the selection and grading of appropriate language material for classroom instruction. The Direct Method did not make much progress because it neglected the above fact. The pioneering work in the preparation of language materials for instruction was carried out at first by a well-known educational psychologist, E.L. Thorndike. According to him for language teaching to be effective and economical, what is to be done is to find out which words are needed most. With this principle in mind he collaborated with Lorge and completed *The Teacher's Wordbook of 30,000 Words* which formed the basis of the word-lists prepared subsequently.[3] However, it soon became evident that vocabulary frequency alone could not be a guiding factor and that the usefulness of a word at a particular stage in the learning of a language also has to be taken into account. The result was Thorndike's *Wordbook,* and *The Interim Report on Vocabulary Selection for Teachers of English as a Foreign Language* prepared by Palmer, Faucett and West in consultation with Thorndike. Later, Michael

West prepared a number of textbooks and supplementary readers based on carefully chosen vocabulary. His aim was to popularise his view that learning to read a foreign language would be easier than learning to speak it. West's method did not become popular because of the exclusive emphasis on reading which made classroom work dull. However, his views constituted a corrective influence on those who advocated the Direct Method and neglected the passive skills in language learning.

A recent method, which has become popular and still holds sway in India, is what may be called the Structural Method. The method has stemmed from the Structural Approach (which we have discussed in an earlier chapter). Palmer is credited with having made a beginning with the Structural Approach. The Structural Approach emphasises the fact that acquiring a command of the basic structures of a language rather than learning words in it is the most important thing in learning the language. The usefulness of vocabulary is limited without a knowledge of basic structures. Palmer's name is generally associated with the Modified Direct Method, but actually his concern was with the practical problems of teaching English as a foreign language. Palmer designed suitable materials for instruction through scientific gradation and insisted on pattern practice or practice in the use of a large number of chosen sentences within a range of controlled vocabulary.[4] The results of his work undertaken in the years before the Second World War are found in his *A Grammar of English Words*. Two others who have continued with the work of Palmer in later years are A.S. Homby and Bruce Pattison. Hornby's *A Guide to Patterns and Usage in English* deserves special mention in this context.

A good deal of work on the Structural Approach has been carried out simultaneously in the USA, too. The contributions of L. Bloomfield and C.C. Fries are significant in this context. Fries describes the Structural Approach in the following words: "The fundamental feature of this new approach to language teaching is a new basis upon which to build the teaching materials. This new approach to the selection and ordering of materials rests upon (a) a scientific descriptive analysis of the language to be learnt, (b) a scientific, descriptive analysis of the language of the learner, (c) a systematic, comparison of these two descriptive analyses in order to bring out completely the difference of structural patterning of the two language systems."[5]

The Structural Method, which is also called the Oral Method, insists that to secure a practical command of English we should know well how the word order, the structural words and the word forms are employed to construct sentences or meaningful patterns of expression. It also insists on graded structures. That is to say, the simple structure must precede the difficult one. In a good syllabus of graded structures, language items to be taught are all set down precisely and in detail. While teaching structures through the Oral Method the student hears the new speech unit from the teacher, recognises it as a series of meaningful sounds, and perhaps understands it. This enables the student to imitate the sounds without analysing individual words, and later to reproduce the structure in an appropriate situation.

The two essential features of the Structural Method are careful grading of structures and vocabulary control. But there are also certain basic assumptions regarding the nature of language and the methods best suited for the presentation of linguistic items. J.B. Bruton in a working paper presented at the Nagpur Seminar in 1958 summarises these assumptions thus: "(a) language is primarily a spoken thing and therefore, our approach to a foreign language should in the first instance be through its spoken forms; (b)... mastery over the signalling system of a language is more important than detailed knowledge of the forms of the language; (c) ... this mastery is best acquired by repetition of the various components of the system in varied forms; (d) ... since language arises from situation, the teacher's task is to create meaningful situations from which language will arise easily and naturally; (e) ... mastery over a given range of structures and confidence in their use are best imparted by concentrating on the teaching of one item at a time; (f) ... each item must be firmly established orally before pupils encounter it in their textbooks.[6] The Structural Syllabus is dependent for its success on the gradation of structures and, therefore, "states which items are to be taught at each stage and goes a step further by indicating the order in which the items should be presented."[7] Bruton lays down the following criteria for the gradation of structures: "(i) area of difference: between the learner's language and English a factor which has to be given due weight in determining the difficulty of various items; (ii) usefulness and teachability: the needs and interests of the pupils at different stages and also certain practical difficulties which may be experienced in creating a proper situation in which a particular structure can be presented; (iii) surrender value: the items cannot be viewed in isolation but as parts of an inter-related course which will ensure a certain mastery over the English language."[8] Besides the grading of structures the Structural Syllabus insists on a basic vocabulary within which the structures should be operated. Thus Bruton maintains that grading of structures and vocabulary control are essential features of the Structural Approach.

The Structural Approach is also called the Structural-cum-Situational Method. A language is best learnt through practice in real situations; this is because of the close relation that exists between experience and expression. The theory is that each structure must be presented in meaningful situations. There are two kinds of situations, artificial and real. Situations can be artificially created or improvised. Appropriate situations may be created by the use of objects in the classroom or outside, by gestures and actions, by the use of pictures and by drawing on the blackboard. We can call these contextually presented situations. Even ideas expressed in words like 'hate', 'love', etc., can be contextualised and presented to the learner. Every structure must be encountered and practised in a context of situation.

It is essential that the structures are drilled properly and repeated in meaningful contexts. The sentence patterns must be practised in illustrative sentences drawn from the students' own experience and activities. Substitution tables must be used to drill the patterns. Individual drill and group drill can be tried. Chorus work also can be attempted. To exact a high standard the teacher has to insist on more and more correctness in each repetition. The procedure that may be followed in the Structural Method is as follows: (a) revision of the previous structure; (b) presentation of the new structure; (c) creating situations to teach the structure; (d) individual/group drill or chorus work; (e) reading from the substitution tables; (f) teaching vocabulary; (g) model reading of the lesson by the teacher; (h) silent reading by the students; (i) comprehension questions; (j) loud reading by the students; (k) composition questions; (1) assignment.

The Structural Method has gained currency in India in recent years, and has been found effective at lower levels. But it is also pointed out that the method is inadequate at the higher levels. Without making any exaggerated claims for the method, we may say that it is quite effective in the hands of trained, dedicated teachers. Inadequate teacher-training has been the cause of the setback the Structural Approach has suffered in India. Effective teaching depends on the teacher and his 'eclectic' ability to adopt and adapt methods and approaches to suit his classroom environment. That is to say, even when his classroom work is mainly based on the Structural Approach, he should be prepared to incorporate into his teaching techniques useful concepts from other approaches and methods. The more knowledge he can have from his study of different approaches, the better he will be able to combine this knowledge with practical experience to produce a suitable teaching methodology for his own purposes. The professional English language teacher should not only have the required personal qualities but also training in the disciplines and fields of study appropriate to the language teaching process.

Apart from the methods and approaches linguists have recommended for the teaching of a second-language, there are certain basic principles common to all good language teaching. No teacher should, however, forget that there is no one method suitable for all occasions and that the teacher cannot decide *a priori* that a particular method is the only one that he must use. What is important for the teacher is to find out what approach and what method will enable him to realise a particular objective under a set of particular circumstances.

According to D.A. Wilkins, there are three basic principles a second-language teacher should follow. The first principle is that he should have clearly defined objectives. The second principle is that once the objectives are realistically defined the classroom activities should be so designed as to realise these objectives. Wilkins says: "When objectives have been defined, the most important principle is to ensure that the linguistic and learning experience is planned so as to be completely representative of the objectives and of the different components of these objectives."[9] This principle is based on the truth that practice makes permanent, though not perfect. Elaborating the principle Wilkins points out that 'we learn what we do' and that experience is all that matters. So, a teacher's duty is to provide a learning experience for his students. The language-learning experience consists of four activities—speaking, listening, reading and writing. These four activities under the guidance of a teacher lead the students to the objectives. That is to say, they are given practice to acquire the skill of speaking intelligibly and acceptably, of listening with understanding, of reading and comprehension and writing with clarity and correctness.

Wilkins while enunciating the second principle speaks of "listening activities to be representative of learning activities" and recommends the "principle of representative proportions."[10] What he means is that the activity in the classroom should be in proportion to the need of the objective: If the need is for listening comprehension then the activity should lay emphasis on this skill rather than on other skills. It is again this principle that should enable the teacher to decide how long spoken language should be taught in preference to the written language and what proportionate importance should be given to speech vis-a-vis writing and to production skills vis-a-vis reception skills.

The third principle which he enunciates is that learners should "model their own language performance on significant instances of target-language behaviour". He further explains: "Language learning will proceed more efficiently if specific instances of language behaviour are modelled for the learner and if he is given ample opportunity to engage in analogous behaviour based on the model provided."[11] Textbooks containing selections of excellent prose writings and teaching aids such as tapes and records prepared by educational experts will come in handy when this principle is put into practice.

The above principles are to a certain extent vague and abstract; they are perhaps more theoretical than practical. But practically useful guidelines for teaching English as a second-language can be deduced from the methods and principles discussed above. These guidelines are catalogued below:

(a) Practice makes permanent; therefore, practice, both oral and written, under the teacher's supervision is necessary for learning to be effective.

(b) Close attention is essential for efficient learning.

(c) Exactimitation is essential; therefore, exposure of the learner to good English should be made possible.

(d) Mistakes, although unavoidable, are harmful. Work should be so organised as to promote the practice of correct English rather than incorrect English.

(e) Mistakes should be corrected as soon as possible.

(f) The systematic eradication of mistakes should follow the principle of dealing with one type of mistake at a time.

(g) Systematic teaching should be reinforced with the help of well-written texts.

(h) The golden rule for the teaching of reading is for the teacher to do nothing for the learner that the learner can safely do for himself.

(i) The above rule is most easily applied when texts are well annotated and glossed or when students are capable of using suitable diction-aries and other works of reference.

(j) A student's English cannot become better than the English he is exposed to.

(k) 'Tough' work which is certain to be done badly should never be set; any assignment given to the learner should be simple enough and should be on the basis of a proper grading.

(1) In a good lesson the teacher may control, direct, counsel and encourage, but the students are at work all the time.

(m) A good teacher almost always tries to get the right answer out of the class before supplying or confirming it himself.

(n) Lecturing does not teach much language.

(o) Correctness of speech rests almost entirely on habit. Correctness of writing rests largely on habit, but writing may be improved (because writing allows time for reflection and checking) by the application of rules and reference to safe models.

(p) For most learners coarse and simple rules are the kind which do most good. Subtleties and complexities are best taught through controlled practice and the demonstration of models.

(q) Demonstration nearly always gets better results than explanation.

(r) Constant evaluation is necessary in order to discover whether the teaching is successful. This does not necessarily steal time from teaching. Many types of evaluation teach as well as test.

(s) Motivation is a basic principle of all kinds of teaching. Positive reinforcement (making correct performance agreeable) is pleasanter for everybody, and usually more effective, than negative reinforcement. Encouragement for correct work, and sympathy, combined with quick and clear correction, when things go wrong, are to be recommended. But inattention or indolence can legitimately be discouraged by downright unpleasantness.

(t) A teacher should never close his eyes to mistakes in expression or failures in comprehension because he feels he must press on through the syllabus. Teaching even two-thirds of the syllabus well will do more good than teaching the whole syllabus badly.

(u) A well-designed examination is a powerful incentive to good teaching and good learning.

References

1. Palmer, H.E., & Palmer, Dorothee, *English Through Actions,* London: Longman, 1959 (*quoted in Teaching English as a Foreign Language* (by J.O. Gauntlett), London: Macmillan, 1966, pp. 17-18

2. Scott, D.H., *Language Teaching in the New Education,* London: University of London Press, 1946, p. 25

3. Thorndike, E.L. & Lorge, I., *The Teacher's Wordbook of 30,000 Words,* Columbia: Columbia University Press, 1944

4. Palmer, H.E., *The Principles of Language Study,* London: George Harrap, 1921, pp. 157-58.

5. Fries, C.C. "American Linguistics and the Teaching of English" in *Language Learning,* Vol. 6, No. 1, 1955

6.   *Report of the Nagpur Seminar,* New Delhi: All India Council of Secondary Education, 1958, p. 46
7.   ibid., p. 44
8.   ibid., p. 43
9.   Wilkins, D.A., *Second-Language Learning and Teaching,* p. 59
10.   ibid., p. 59
11.   ibid., pp. 69-70

For Further Reading

1.   Dodd, W.A., *The Teacher at Work,* Oxford: Oxford University Press, 1970
2.   Halliday, M.A.K., etc., *The Linguistic Sciences and Language Teaching,* London: Longman, 1964
3.   Homsey, Alan, W., (ed.) *Handbook for Modern Language Teachers,* London: Methuen, 1975
4.   Rivers, W.M., *Teaching Foreign Language Skills,* Chicago: University of Chicago Press, 1969

SEVEN

HOW TO TEACH ENGLISH PRONUNCIATION

We have already noticed that there are varieties of English and that we, Indian learners of English, aim at learning to speak a variety of English that is the most widely acceptable and intelligible and that attracts the least attention to itself. In other words, the Indian student's aim to learn to speak and write a normal or Standard English which follows what is commonly called Received Pronunciation or RP. According to Quirk RP is often associated with Public Schools, Oxford and the BBC. But he also remarks: "Indeed, a pronunciation within this range has great prestige throughout the world, and for English taught as a foreign language it is more usually the ideal than any other pronunciation."[1]

The terms 'Standard English' and 'Received Pronunciation' stand for such use of English as that which does not reveal any regional peculiarities. This does not, however, mean that Standard English or Received Pronunciation has any absolute values; for every individual speaker of a language has his own peculiarities even within Standard English or Received Pronunciation. It is these peculiarities that enable us to identify an individual from his speech or from his writing. An individual's language habits are termed his idiolect, and these habits are peculiar to him as an individual. What is meant by Standard English or RP, however, refers to "the body of relatively homogeneous usage which marks the speech of educated people as alike, and which is referred to as Received Pronunciation (in reference to speech sounds) and Standard English (in reference to word usage and grammatical forms)".[2]

Teaching pronunciation is fundamental to the teaching of listening and speaking. Therefore, it is necessary that the teacher of English in India should pay a good deal of attention to pronunciation. That is to say, the second-language learner should be trained to respond to a totally new sound system. But it should be remembered that this training should be set in a context of genuine language use; for continuous speech is understood by the listener not merely because of his knowledge of the pronunciation of individual words but also because of his ability to understand vocabulary, grammar and contextual meaning. So, the first point to remember while teaching pronunciation is that the drilling of isolated sounds alone has only a limited value. What is important is to teach pronunciation of words used in continuous speech.

The next point to note is that effective teaching of pronunciation is not possible without the teacher having equipped himself with some background knowledge of phonology and phonetics. This is not to impart this knowledge directly to the students but to know what to teach them. Phonology deals with the sound system and phonetics with the physical properties of sounds and their place and manner of articulation in the vocal track.

Sounds used in a language are distinctive. It is this fact that enables us to distinguish them from each other. Thus cap is distinguished from *sap* and *sap* from *sop*. This difference of sound is called phonemic difference; the phonemes involved here are /k/, /s/, /a/, /o/, and /p/. In English there are twenty-three consonant phonemes and twenty-one vowel phonemes (including dipthongs). A phoneme is the smallest contrastive unit that may bring about a change of meaning. It is the difference between the phonemes/b/and/p/that makes bit and pit mean different things. An awareness of the phonemic and allophonic differ- ences enables the student to distinguish between such minimal pairs as the following:

ship	sheep
cart	curt
hard	heard
star	stir
feet	fit
barn	burn
pin	spin
kill	skill

The teacher's knowledge of phonology should not be confined to English phonology alone; it should extend to that of the student's mother tongue too. If he is capable of listing the phonemes of English and comparing them with those of his students' first language (or mother tongue), then he will be able to do a lot of remedial work by trying to undo old habits.

The structure of the sound system of a language involves stress and intonation also. These, unlike the vowels and consonants (which are the segmental features), are the supra-segmental features. Stress is emphasis, loudness or force; it functions partly phonemically in words, and partly as a feature of longer phrases or sentences. That is to say, stress functions within a word with one or more syllables having heavier stress and at phrase or sentence level with one or more words stressed more heavily than others. Consider, for example, the sentence, "I expect you tomorrow morning". If the stress is on the phrase "tomorrow morning" then the sentence means that "tomorrow morning" and not any other time "you" are expected. If the stress is on "you", the speaker implies that "you" are expected, and none else.

The function of intonation is to convey attitudinal or emotional meaning and is very closely associated with the context of an utterance. Thus "Please go away" can sound pleading or peremptory depending on the intonation used. The teacher of English as a second-language should see that in the course of his instruction he draws the attention of the class to these supra-segmental aspects of an utterance.

The teacher's knowledge of the phonology of English should also extend to a knowledge of phonetics. This will enable him to train his students in pronouncing each word with the stress or accent on the right syllable and in pronouncing the words in a sentence with fluency and ease paying heed to the appropriate juncture. The aim of pronunciation teaching is to help the students produce English speech which is intelligible and acceptable. The teacher need not, however, aim at phonetic perfection; he will have to concentrate on the important phonemic contrasts and select allophonic variations so that intelligibility is ensured. For instance, he should see that his students pronounce 'state' (steit) and 'estate' (isteit), 'rate' (reit) and 'raid' (reid) and similar pairs of words distinctively.

Teaching pronunciation is most neglected in the teaching of English in India. Perhaps this is partly due to the teacher's lack of competence and partly due to inattention and indifference. So, it is necessary that the teacher develops an ability to handle broad transcription, if not narrow transcription, and acquires a knowledge of the principles underlying such transcription. It is a moot point whether or not the students who are already familiar with conventional spelling should also know the phonetic script. Perhaps familiarity with the script on their part is useful in following the transcription given by the teacher to the class. The students, unless they happen to be teacher-trainees, need not, however, be taught the fundamentals of phonetics as such.

A list of English sounds and keywords with their phonetic transcriptions is available in *The Advanced Learner's Dictionary of Current English* and Daniel Jones's *English Pronouncing Dictionary.* The students should be encouraged to use these books often enough.

The most important technique in teaching pronunciation is imitation—some kind of intuitive mimicry on the part of students. That is to say, the teacher's pronunciation of the word that is taught should be closely imitated by the students through the process of repetition and practice. As Leonard Bloomfield rightly says, "The command of a language is not a matter of knowledge.... (It) is a matter of practice."[3]

As already suggested pronunciation teaching should not stop at the drilling of pronunciation of individual words; it should extend to the recognition and use of the sound feature in normal speech. This is possible only if attention is paid to the supra-segmental aspects of pronunciation—intonation, stress and juncture. So, practice in repeating patterns of sentences as part of the training in pronunciation should be attempted in class. This is of particular importance because of native language interference which applies equally strongly to both the segmental and supra-segmental aspects of pronunciation.

Pronunciation teaching has to be done in the course of teaching class texts. It is perhaps difficult to have a graded teaching sequence for this. It is for individual teachers to decide on priorities and degrees of difficulty and slip a few minutes' pronunciation drill into a lesson. For instance, in a grammar class pronunciation practice with plural endings, third person singular simple present tense, simple past tense and past participles of regular verbs, etc., may be tried usefully.

A few key principles in pronunciation practice recommended by Geoffrey Broughton and his collaborators in their book, *Teaching English as a Foreign Language*, have been found useful and are reproduced below:

1. Recognition practice should precede production practice.
2. But since production reinforces recognition, there is no need to wait for perfect recognition before asking for production.
3. The sounds to be heard and spoken should be clearly highlighted in short utterances.
4. But this should not be taken to the extreme of tongue-twisters like Peter Piper.
5. Students should be given the opportunity to hear the same things said by more than one voice as the model.

6.   The English sounds can be demonstrated with other English sounds or else in contrast with sounds from the native language.
7.   The target sound contrast should be shown to function meaningfully, i.e. "students should realise that it makes an important difference to their intelligibility to use it properly."[4]

The reason why pronunciation teaching in English is important is that the orthography of English words is unphonetic and that of our own languages is phonetic. Our students often tend to pronounce words following the spellings of words, perhaps owing to the influence of their mother tongue; this results in mispronunciation. The influence of the mother tongue is also felt in the supra-segmentals like stress, intonation and juncture. Teaching pronunciation and making the students pronunciation-conscious constitute a corrective measure. What is to be borne in mind is that though pronunciation is not to be regarded as a separate area of language learning, yet it is necessary that teachers and students give their attention to it from time to time.

References

1.   Quirk, Randolph, *The Use of English,* pp. 91-92
2.   Wallwork, J.F., *Language and Linguistics,* p. 104
3.   Bloomfield, Leonard, *Outline Guide for the Practical Study of Foreign Languages,* Baltimore; Linguistics Society of America, 1942, p.12
4.   Broughton, Geoffrey & Others, *Teaching English as a Foreign Language,* p. 62

For Further Reading

1.   Amold, G.F. & Gimson, A.C., *English Pronunciation Practice,* London: Hodder and Stoughton, 1965
2.   Bolinger, D. (ed.), *Intonation,* Hammondsworth: Penguin, 1972
3.   Cook, V.J., *Active Intonation,* Longman: 1968
4.   Gimson, A.G., *An Introduction to the Pronunciation of English,* Amold, 1970
5.   Haycraft, B., *The Teaching of English Pronunciation: A Classroom Guide,* Longman, 1970
6.   Heliel, M. and McArthur, T.,: *Learning Rhythm and Stress,* Collins, 1974
7.   O'Connor, J.D. and Arnold, G.F., *Better English Pronunciation,* Cambridge University Press, 1967
8.   Trim J., *English Pronunciation Illustrated,* Cambridge University Press, 1975

EIGHT

TEACHING THE FOUR SKILLS

Learning a second language is in effect learning the four skills, viz. listening speaking, reading and writing. The first two skills are intimately related to each other, though one is a recognition skill and the other is a production skill. Also, both skills depend almost entirely on the learner's knowledge of the pronunciation of words and the articulation of sounds in the language.

(i) Listening

Familiarity with the English sound system and an ability to articulate English sounds prepare the students for listening to English utterances with understanding. And listening that should precede speaking paves the way for them to develop oral fluency and accuracy. Listening is often said to be a passive skill while speaking is described as an active one. This is not wholly true; for listening is also an active skill as it is concerned with decoding a message and understanding it; moreover the listener has to show that he has or has not understood the message from his response. Listening is a skill that can be developed through systematic teaching.

Listening ability can be cultivated through listening practice, both extensive and intensive. Extensive listening implies exposure to a wide variety of structures and sounds. This equips the students to listen with understanding to English later in real life situations. Intensive listening is concerned with just one or two specific points; this kind of listening practice is primarily for language items as part of the language teaching programme. Both kinds of practice can be done with the help of the recordings which the teacher makes himself as well as with the tapes that accompany texts like Crystal and Davy's *Advanced Conversational English*. At a more sophisticated level this can be done in the language laboratory. The point is that the students must listen to good models. Listening is found to be most effective when it is done in preparation for speaking.

In India our students are hampered in their ability to listen for meaning by certain weaknesses. In general these weaknesses are:

(a)   inadequate range of words and phrases that are understood;
(b)   inability to maintain attention;
(c)   inability to understand pronunciation other than the personal or regional pronunciation;
(d)   inability to understand fast speech;
(e)   inability to understand against background noise through acoustic/ electrical interference.

The main remedy for the first weakness lies in the student enriching, his vocabulary through reading and by looking up unfamiliar words in: dictionaries with phonetic transcriptions such as *The Advanced Learner's Dictionary of Current English.*

The second weakness is general. Many efficient listeners for short stretches lose their efficiency if they have to go on listening for an unbroken stretch of more than twenty minutes. It has been found from experience that dictation is an admirable exercise for sharpening attention. Listening to broadcasts or recordings of full-length plays, and to films, is almost certainly of great value. The dramatic situation and the variety of dialogue combine to maintain interest, and hence attention, even over long stretches.

Remedy for the third weakness is to be sought in learning the correct pronunciation of each word. This is possible with the help of a pronouncing dictionary like Daniel Jones's *English Pronouncing Dictionary* and by listening to recordings, broadcasts and dialogues in films.

The teacher can deal with the fourth weakness by adjusting his speech and clarity to the capacity of the class and gradually speeding up. When the context makes vivid the meaning, it becomes easy for the students to follow even fast speech. This fact and the interest of the action that sharpens attention in plays and films, for instance, enable people to follow fast speech without difficulty.

It is practically very important for everyone in this electronic age to listen with understanding against background noise. So, the fifth weakness has to be dealt with seriously; tape-recorders and specially prepared recordings are indispensable for this, unless the whole thing is left to chance experience. A tape-recorder is even otherwise a valuable aid in much of the remedial work connected with the teaching of the four language skills.

There are many exercises which the teacher himself can devise for doing remedial work. One such exercise for developing all-round efficiency in listening is the answering of multiple-choice questions on pieces that have been heard. One can start by setting single questions on single spoken sentences, and work up through pieces of steadily increasing length.

(ii) Speaking

We have seen that practice in listening should precede practice in speaking. At the phonological level this is particularly helpful; the students should be able to recognise a sound before they attain an ability to produce it. But listening does not lead naturally on to speaking and oral fluency in communication unless listening is followed by practice at the grammatical and lexical levels too. So, listening-attention should be sharpened with particular emphasis on grammatical and lexical items. (Listening is a receptive skill like reading and speaking is a productive skill like writing. Just as sharpening reading-attention benefits writing, sharpening listening-attention benefits speaking.)

While giving practice in speaking, the teacher may start with dialogues. Dialogues on simple, contextualised situations may be tried between pair of students. The teacher should control and guide the students without curbing their freedom of expression. This will give the students enough opportunities to practice certain phonological, grammatical and lexical items.

Reading aloud is another technique usually employed for teaching oral English. The practice is for one of the students to read aloud a passage and the others to review his reading critically through interrupting him and requiring him to repeat a word or phrase. The technique, however, is objectionable on psychological and pedagogical grounds. It provides practice only to a few students and bores everybody else. It can be embarrassing to the reader in so far as it tends to make him self-conscious. It interferes with the proper business of the reading lesson which is to increase the reading speed instead of slowing it. The practice is random, and not specific. The material chosen from a book is not generally connected with situations that can generate the interest of the class in general. So, reading aloud probably does little good in teaching the skill of speaking unless it is done really well so as to hold the attention and interest of the whole class. It is almost certainly better to practice a weak student hard at reading one or two sentences aloud and getting him to read this short stretch really well in the end, calling attention only to the mispronunciation here and there than to let him read aloud a long paragraph badly. In dealing with a short stretch, there is the advantage that the practice can quickly move around the class, and involve the attention and activity of every student.

The teacher who gives practice in oral English will find it useful if he has sufficient skill in phonetic transcription to write down at once a mispronunciation that he hears. An elementary knowledge of general articulatory phonetics is also useful to the teacher. This enables him to know what is actually going wrong when a faulty articulation produces a faulty sound. While there is no need for students to memorise or be able to write a phonetic transcription, they should at any rate be able to read a glossary/dictionary/blackboard transcription with the aid of a key. Even understanding stress-marks which may be used with ordinary orthography is far better than having no familiarity with transcription and articulatory phonetics.

As already mentioned, intelligibility and acceptability should be our aims in teaching spoken English. Particular attention should, therefore, be paid to the following drawbacks generally noticed in our students:

(a) misplaced stress on syllables and words or absence of stress at all:
(b) confusion between sound with meaningful contrasts (e.g./bit/v./bit/);
(c) failure to discriminate between long and short vowels or diphthongs;
(d) interference of the phonological system of the mother tongue of the learner;
(e) failure to aspirate initial /p/,/t/, and /k/;
(f) a tendency to aspirate/h/ when not required;
(h) production of the harsh sounds /r/ in words like 'wonderful', 'far', etc.;
(i) misapplication of lexis and idiom.

The reasons for the unacceptability of an utterance have been given in Chapter 2 of this book and need not be repeated here. However, it should be borne in mind that an otherwise intelligible utterance becomes unacceptable because of grammatical, lexical, syntactic and idiomatic inaccuracies and that the concatenation of blunders which seem, on first analysis, to be trivial matters of non-acceptability may sometimes lead to downright unintelligibility.

What is important is that a student who learns English as a second-language should be able to feel that he has the basic; machinery to say what he wants. It is not an easy thing to instill this confidence in the student; it calls for considerable preparation and creative thought on the part of the teacher.

(iii)Reading

Reading like listening is a decoding process. But it is a very complex process involving many physical, intellectual and often emotional reactions. Moreover, it entails the ability to recognise graphic symbols and their corresponding vocal sounds. It is impossible to learn to read without this ability which extends to complex groups of sounds called words, phrases, sentences, paragraphs and chapters. In other words, there are three important components in the reading skill: these are the recognition of the graphic marks, the correlation of these with formal linguistic elements, and the correlation of these with meaning. Reading becomes meaningful only if we get at the meaning behind the graphic symbols through our ability to recognise the semantic content of the graphic symbols and the sounds they represent.

There are two kinds of reading skill: the skill of reading aloud and the skill of reading silently. Reading aloud is primarily an oral matter; it is closer to pronunciation than to comprehension. It is good that the students develop the skill of reading aloud. However, only a few people are required to 'read aloud as a matter of daily routine; newscasters, teachers, actors, etc., are some of them who should cultivate the skill; the huge majority do not have to read aloud except on occasions. This is not so with silent reading. The greatest amount of reading that is done in the world is silent. The skill of silent reading, however, varies from person to person and depends on several factors including each person's requirement.

Broadly speaking, there are five uses of silent reading. These are: (1) to make a survey of materials to be studied and to look through indexes, chapter headings and outlines, (2) to skim, (3) to familiarise oneself with the material and its thought content, (4) to study the material in depth, and (5) to study the language in which the material is written from a literary or linguistic point of view.

The second-language teacher should pay special attention to silent reading. (He may for other reasons such as teaching pronunciation, articulation of sounds etc. devote his attention to the training of his students in loud reading.) This is because the student who wants to learn English will have to read a lot so as to have a knowledge of the language, and only silent reading enables him to do it at some speed. Moreover, all the important study skills require quick, efficient and imaginative reading, and this is possible in silent reading rather than in loud reading.

Reading becomes easy to the student if he is trained to comprehend the patterns of relationships between words—'the semantic patterns of lexical items'. These patterns of relationships are mainly three: (1) the relationship that exists between the author and his text, (2) the relationship that exists between the reader and the text, and (3) the relationship that exists between the text and the culture. So, good silent reading presupposes a knowledge of the cultural value of words and expressions and the ability to identify the thematic content of what is in the text. This means that while teaching the mechanics of silent reading the teacher should be very careful in selecting the material for his students to read. The material should not go over their heads in respect of any of the above relationships.

The mechanics of reading should be taught to the students. They should be trained to increase the speed of their reading. There are three simple rules which they should be made to follow. These are: (1) while reading there should not be any muscular articulation; lips and tongue should be kept still; (2) word for word reading should be avoided in favour of taking in meaningful groups or units of words; (3) the head must be kept still while the eyes rove steadily from left to right and only swing back to the left again at the end of the row without any movement of the head. In other words, the first attempt of the teacher should be to enable his students to improve their visual perception of words and phrases. Exercises may be designed by him for rapid word identification, rapid phrase identification and rapid recognition of meaning. The book, *Teaching Faster Reading*, by Edward Fry gives sound guidance in this regard. The simplest technique of improving speed is to use a series of graded, sequenced and varied texts for silent reading and to test the students understanding of them by means of multiple-choice questions.

We have observed that there are five kinds of silent reading. The first three of them, viz. survey reading, skimming, and superficial reading come under extensive reading while the last two, viz. content study reading and linguistic or literary study come under intensive reading. Extensive reading presupposes speed and ease which come only from copious reading. One of the drawbacks of instruction in English in our educational institutions is that no encouragement in the form of facilities is given to the students to read copiously. As a remedial step, students should be introduced to a graded list of simple or simplified novels and biographies, and questions regarding the names of the main characters, the nature of the story etc. which do not require critical or analytical answers may be set for them.

Intensive reading has for its objective the full understanding of the text with its argument, its symbolic, emotional and social overtones, the attitudes and purposes of the author and the linguistic and literary means the author employs to achieve his purpose. Intensive reading in a sense is study. There is a misunderstanding that study and slow reading are the same. Study involves several other skills besides reading as well as several kinds of reading skill. A good student perhaps makes a survey at first of the book he is going to study, and consequently, has to resort to skimming occasionally while reading intensively. Students will also have to develop study skills such as reading, recording, and revising and it is here that skimming, reading for specific points of information and practice in formulating pertinent questions come in handy.

On the basis of what has been given above we may say that an efficient reader must possess the following skills:

(a) ability to read fast and with good comprehension texts that are easy in language and content, or difficult texts that are familiar;
(b) ability to read slowly, but with excellent comprehension, difficult texts on professional, academic and technical subjects in which he has a special interest and requires specialised knowledge;
(c) ability to skim and dip;
(d) ability to use works of reference;
(e) ability to size up a book quickly.

In the classroom the teacher should test the students in all these skills and remedial treatment applied to weaknesses, if any. One common weakness is for readers, whose comprehension is good, to read with quite unnecessary slowness. Sometimes childish physical habits may be slowing them down—e.g. pointing or mouthing—or they may simply have formed the habit of reading silently at about the same slow pace as that of reading aloud. Again, faulty eye-movements may be either a symptom or cause of slowness. Slowness in reading may be a symptom of sheer lack of interest in reading. This is a serious weakness as it affects the study of the subject itself as well as the ability to acquire general education. The best cure is to find easy texts which are likely to prove particularly interesting to the sufferer from this weakness.

Difficult intensive reading is quite a different matter from easy fast reading. Here faults tend to be
(a) misunderstanding of word-meanings that strictly follow definitions;
(b) incomplete or faulty understanding of concepts.

Weaknesses in intensive reading of the above kind may be effectively dealt with by carefully derived multiple-choice questions. With intelligent students, such tests, if they reveal weaknesses, may be usefully followed up by re-examination of the text and discussions based on it.

A person who cannot skim and dip is severely handicapped in his handling of the printed word. Training in skimming and dipping is easy to give. What is to be done in class is to demand quick answers relating to widely separated points in the text which students are asked to read in a specified time. It is quite a good exercise to make a student find a particular news item in a newspaper and tell the teacher what it is.

The use of works of reference is largely a matter of skill in alphabetical location. It is surprising to note that many people, even educated native speakers, are poor at this. Controlled practice cures this weakness. Telephone directories and dictionaries offer good practice material. A minute or two of practice in the occasional lesson may prevent a lot of time-wasting. Systematic training should be given in the quick location of needed materials.

If a student cannot size up a book quickly and accurately he must be trained to do so. He must learn to get his clues from such things as title, author, date, publisher, blurb, list of contents, index and thorough quick skimming.

(iv) Writing

Learning to write a second-language is not merely learning to put down on paper the conventional symbols of the writing system that represents the utterances one has in mind, but it is also purposeful selection and organisation of ideas, facts, and/or experience. In other words, writing is a thinking process and is much more than an exercise in transcription or copying.

Writing is different from speaking in that it aims at compactness and precision in expression as well as grammatical, idiomatic and ortho-graphic accuracy and in that conventions of writing tend to be less flexible than those of speech. Moreover, the student who learns to write English has not only to cope with the mechanical problems connected with the script of the language but also with the problems of ease and fluency of expression, of grammatical and lexical accuracy and of the appropriateness of the style of writing as demanded by the occasion or situation. Learning to write, therefore, is learning to use grammar with ease and facts in some sequential order as tools. This definition of learning to write leads us to the question how we should set about the task.

Since composition or writing involves both accuracy and fluency, the problem arises which of them should be the first goal. There are some "who believe that fluency must be given priority over accuracy and that the student should be encouraged to produce extensively with little regard to the number and type of errors and infelicities he may make."[1] Perhaps this is not an acceptable point of view in the context of English teaching in India. We should aim at both accuracy and fluency. We should expect our students to master the elementary mechanics of written work, viz. handwriting, spelling, capitalisation, punctuation, word order and word division (all within the range of the vocabulary and structures they have learnt), and sentence structure and constructions before they are given a free hand to develop ease and fluency in writing.

Keeping in mind the above, we may say that a writing course for the students who have reached the intermediate level may consist of the following three stages: (1) controlled writing, (2) guided writing, and (3) free writing. Controlled writing may be distinguished from guided writing in that the former concerns itself with structures, use of appropriate words, punctuations, word order etc., and not with facts or ideas while the latter concerns itself with ideas and facts supplied by the teacher for the students to express in their own sentences observing the mechanics of composition. That is to say, filling in the blanks in a paragraph or answering questions based on a picture in which the teacher gives facts or ideas in the form of an outline and thus assists the students is a guided composition. In a free composition the teacher gives only the title and it is for the students to decide on the facts he should include and their arrangement and expression in some logical sequence. In the words of Geoffrey Broughton and others, "Generally the controlled stage concerns itself with the production of accurate language in context, the guided stage with the organisation of material which is given, and the free stage with the production by the student of both content and language."[2]

The main aims of a writing course are to train the student in expressing himself effectively in good English. That is to say, "he must be taught to present his information in a format acceptable for the occasion, be that an informal friendly letter or a matter-of-fact business communication, a report to the teacher or an article for publication."[3] The student should, therefore, be "taught to be sensitive to the rules of discourse in English" as well as to "obey certain conventions which are appropriate to the particular purpose"[4] he has in mind. In short, the language used by him should be good and effective, and suit the matter that is conveyed as well as the occasion for which it is composed.

The question may now be asked: what should be the syllabus of a writing course? The answer is that it may consist of exercises varying from controlled and guided paragraph writing to free writing of essays on familiar topics. It may include all kinds of letter writing, report writing, etc. Dictation is also a form of written exercise, though as an effective teaching device it has often been neglected. The importance of dictation arises from the fact that many of the errors made by students are due to confusion about the orthographic system and that dictation is an effective way of correcting these errors. Dictation can be either word dictation or text dictation. One big advantage of dictation as an exercise is that it can be used with a class of any size and the student gets practice not only in writing but also in the sort of note-taking that many courses require.

Whether or not precis-writing should form part of a writing course is, however, a moot point. Perhaps the traditional type of precis-writing exercise in which the student is required to summarise the passage in his own words in the third person reducing it to one-third of its original length poses difficulties and problems and does not serve the purpose it is intended for. As J.A. Bright and G.P. McGregor rightly say: "The precis question was popular with examiners because it was easy to set, easy to mark, and an excellent test of skill in the manipulation of words. But for students for whom English was a second-language it was not even this."[5] The precis question, if treated as a mere exercise in summarising, may, however, serve a useful purpose as a kind of composition.

Whatever be the kind of exercise set for the students, some guidelines such as the following are useful:

(a) the composition course should cover the widest possible range of kinds of writing;

(b) the teacher must see that progress is achieved in successive stages and that anything more demanding than the earlier stage is set only after ensuring that progress has been achieved in the previous stage;

(c) no exercise should be set that is too difficult for the student; any task that is assigned to the student should be adjusted in its presentation to an appropriate level of difficulty and should be capable of being tackled within the language the student knows;

(d) whatever grammar teaching that is done should be relevant to the needs of composition;

(e) all composition work should draw on the student's own experience;

(f) the teacher should not do anything for a student that he can do for himself;

(g) the student should be encouraged to write a draft of the exercise first, revise it and then rewrite it.

The suggestions given by Geoffrey Broughton and others for the teacher to bring the task to the level of the class are useful; according to them, the teacher can "(i) limit the length of the written material to be produced, (ii) increase the amount of class preparation for the task, (iii) provide guidance on the final form of the written work, for example with picture prompts, or word prompts as a result of the oral preparation, (iv) encourage students to collaborate in the actual process of writing, (v) allow cross-checking between the draft stage and the writing of the final product, (vi) limit the complexity of the writing task itself, and (vii) can demand that the task be completed either slowly or quickly."[6]

The students' written work should be gone through by the teacher. This will enable him to assess the students' level of achievement and prepare for the tasks ahead. But what should be the teacher's approach to composition correction? Should he mark every error or should he be selective, and should he merely underline the mistakes without effecting any correction? The traditional practice has been for the teacher to mark every error in red ink and draw the attention of the student to the errors. This practice is nowadays viewed with disfavour because it is likely to dampen the student's enthusiasm for the study of the language. As J.A. Bright and G.P. McGregor observe: "The teacher who carefully crosses out or underlines every mistake in his pupils' books develops a keen eye for errors but his pupils do not: it is easier for them to develop a tolerance of red-ink rash. It is the pupils and not the teacher who should learn to spot mistakes by practising proof-reading." In their view the teacher should never do anything for the student that the student can do for himself. So, their suggestion is that the teacher should use symbols in the margin of the exercise book against the mistakes committed by the student so that he may attempt to correct them himself, or if he fails, seek the help of the teacher."[7] The teacher, for instance, may indicate spelling mistakes by 'S', mistakes in the use of tense by 'T', wrong construction by 'C', grammatical error by 'G', etc. and also direct the student occasionally to consult a dictionary by using 'D'.

Donald Knapp goes one step further in his suggestion. He offers a check list for use in the classroom; his basic assumptions are: "...composition teachers aren't proof-readers and shouldn't be;... it is a mistake in itself to mark all the mistakes; ... the correction of grammatical errors is only a subsidiary aim in teaching composition;; ...giving a composition a grade is unnecessary and undesirable."[8] The check list should cover those items which the teacher expects the student to have assimilated, and if his composition shows that he has used an item successfully a red plus may be marked in front of the item on the composition check list; this will be a kind of encouragement to the student. The check list will also be useful to the teacher to direct the student's attention to the items which he has not assimilated by singling them out and explaining them to the student with the help of correct patterns.

What is important in correction work is the student's active participation. The teacher's explanation in class and the painstaking manner in which he marks the mistakes will yield results only if the student works for himself by correcting the mistakes. In other words, the student should be made to write out all corrections in full. If the exercise is written on alternate lines, the student can neatly cross out and correct, and achieve a text which says in good English what he was trying to say in the first place. Error analysis on the basis of the composition check list suggested by Donald Knapp may be done. A limited number of classified categories are enough at a time, but the treatment of one category needs the scrutiny and analysis of mistakes in that category.

Besides correcting the student's composition, the teacher should take practical steps to remedy the weaknesses in writing generally seen in a composition class. These weaknesses are:
(a)   inadequacy of lexical range;
(b)   misapplications of words and phrases;
(c)   grammatical faults;
(d)   mis-spellings;
(e)   faulty punctuation;
(f)   use of words that are outdated.

The main cure for these weaknesses is reading contemporary English. The student should be made to realise that the good writer, native or non-native, is a constant reader. As suggested above error analysis is essential to the diagnosis of grammatical faults and to the assessment of the efficacy of remedial treatment. The best cure for grammatical faults is intensive drilling—oral drilling first and then written exercises. Explanation supported by models and pradigms too has its value when the grammatical principle is easy to grasp. Poor writers may be greatly helped by being made, and given time, to follow a simple system of checks, set out on reasonably short stencilled handouts.

References

1.   Erazmus, Edward, T., "Second Language Composition Teaching at Intermediate Level" (quoted on p. 265 of *Teaching English as a Second Language,* edited by Harold B. Allen)
2.   Broughton, Geoffrey & Others, *Teaching English as a Foreign Language,* p. 119
3.   Lado, Robert, *Language Teaching,* p. 146
4.   Broughton, Geoffrey & Others, ibid., p. 120

5. Bright, J.A. & McGregor, G.P., *Teaching English as a Second Language,* p. 169
6. Broughton, Geoffrey & Others, ibid., p. 121
7. Bright, J.A. & McGregor, G.P., ibid., pp. 154-55
8. Knapp, Donald, "A Focused Efficient Method to Relate Composition Correction to Teaching Aims" in *Teaching English as a Second Language* edited by Harold B. Allen & Russell N. Campbell, Bombay: Tata McGraw-Hill, 1965, p. 213

For Further Reading

1. Brittan K., *Advanced Listening Comprehension Practice in English,* Hamish Hamilton, 1974
2. Brown, G., *Listening to Spoken English,* Longman, 1977
3. Byme, D., *Teaching Oral English,* Longman, 1976.
4. Chaplen, F., *Communication Practice in Spoken English,* Oxford University Press, 1975
5. Combe Martin, M.H. *Listening and Comprehending,* Macmillan, 1970
6. Crystal, D. and Davy, D., *Advanced Conversational English,* Longman, 1976
7. Fry, E., *Teaching Faster Reading,* Cambridge University Press, 1963
8. George, H.V., *Common Errors in English Learning,* Newbury House, 1972
9. Hartog, P. & Others, *The Making of English Essays,* Macmillan, 1941
10. Jupp, T.C. and Milne, J., *Guided Course in English Composition,* Heinemann, 1968
11. Jupp, T.C. and Milne J., *Guided Paragraph Writing,* Heinemann, 1972
12. Moon, C. and Raban, B., *A Question of Reading,* Ward Lock, 1975

NINE

HOW TO TEACH VOCABULARY

The teaching of vocabulary is as important as the teaching of structures. A thorough familiarity with the syntax of English and an ability to use the basic structures of the language are a prerequisite, but equally important is a command of words. This is because language is meant for communication and it is in words that concepts and ideas are enshrined. Without the use of meaningful words no communication is possible. The teaching of vocabulary is, however, a difficult task. Different methods are to be employed at different stages of proficiency, and at each stage an attempt should be made to facilitate the learning process on the part of the student. This is likely to be tedious, especially when the class consists of a large number of students.

Words used in a language constitute its vocabulary. Broadly speaking, there are two classifications of words. These are: (i) function words, and (ii) content words. Function words are interrogatives, prepositions, auxiliaries, etc., and content words are those words of particular grammatical classes that are meaningful. Fries, however, classifies English words into four groups, namely, (i) function words or structural words, (ii) substitute words, (iii) grammatically distributed words, and (iv) content words.[1] According to him, substitute words replace a class and several sub-classes of words. By 'grammatically distributed words'. he refers to words like 'some', 'any', which "show unusual grammatical restrictions in distribution". The first three categories number about 200 in all. It is content words that constitute the bulk of vocabulary.

Content words can be divided into two. One is a common core vocabulary, generally known to the members of a language community; the other consists of specialised vocabularies. On the basis of this distinction of content words, Robert Lado speaks of three levels of vocabulary: "(i) vocabulary to operate the patterns and illustrate the pronunciation of the language, (ii) vocabulary for communication in areas of wide currency, and (iii) aesthetic and technical vocabularies."[2] The third level of vocabulary is specialised, and is not generally the concern of the student of English as a second-language in India, unless he becomes a professional student. But the other two levels of vocabulary which constitute a common core vocabulary should be very much his concern as he has to learn to use the language for purposes of communication.

Vocabulary is also divided into recognition vocabulary and production vocabulary. This division is based on the fact that the vocabulary which we can actually recognise but do not ourselves use for purposes of communication is much larger than the vocabulary which enables us to communicate in ordinary situations. The vocabulary that conveys meaning to us is our recognition vocabulary, and the vocabulary that is used by us for communication is our production vocabulary. What is referred to as the production vocabulary is the student's active vocabulary (i.e. the vocabulary he is expected to use in speaking and writing); recognition vocabulary is his passive vocabulary (i.e. the vocabulary he recognises when spoken to or while reading). As he advances in his studies, much of the initially passive vocabulary becomes active until finally only specialised and technical words remain passive (and that too, if he is not getting technically qualified).

Fries defines a word as "a combination of sounds acting as a stimulus to bring into attention the experience to which it has become attached by use."[3] A word thus has a meaning attached to it. This meaning of the word changes depending on the experience it conveys in the context and the collocation of words in which it is used. For example, 'bar' has different meanings depending on the contexts in which it is used; it may mean 'a rod or oblong piece', 'a broad line or band', 'a bolt', 'a counter across which drinks are served' or 'barristers as a whole'. So too, when a chartered accountant speaks of 'going through the books', he does not mean the same as when a teacher of English says that he has to 'go through some books'.

The meaning of a word is not always the dictionary meaning or what it literally denotes. What the word connotes in a particular context is more important than its denotation and is sometimes the only meaning warranted by the context in which it is used. Connotation is the implication of something more than the accepted or primary meaning and refers to the qualities, attributes and characteristics suggested by the word. For example, the word 'dictatorship' denotes 'a form of government controlled by an individual', but it connotes (for the people of democratic countries, any way) brutality, ruthlessness, injustice etc.

The question basic to the teaching of vocabulary is: how should we teach our students vocabulary? We cannot teach them vocabulary direct. This is because it is not always possible to identify the meaning of a word outside some other kind of contexts and also because the meaning of a word is determined by the other words in the contexts, that is, by collocation. For example, 'a run on the bank' is different from 'a thief on the run'. Vocabulary lessons that emphasise learning facts about words independent of the contexts in which they are used in sentences do not yield the right kind of results; for the student fails to understand the different collocational and connotative possibilities of the words. Moreover, our lessons should aim at teaching the students not merely lexis but also grammatical patterns of the language. So, the first thing that we have to bear in mind is that vocabulary has to be taught from textbooks in which the use of words is contextualised.

The second point relates to the number of words that are required to be taught to a second-language learner so that he may have the basic competence for speaking, listening, reading and writing. This point is important because unless we have some kind of selection and control, we are in grave danger of being lost in the jungle of words. Selection presupposes an assessment of the ability of the average learner to learn. The criteria of selection are mainly frequency and range.

The frequency with which a word is used in normal reading matter is perhaps an objective standard by which to judge the importance of the word. The more frequently used a word is, the more useful it is; also, the more frequently used a word is, the more easily will it be remembered. This is why frequency becomes important. 'Range' refers to the frequency of a word used in a variety of situations. Structural words, certain types of adverbs, adjectives, verbs and abstract nouns are generally words having a very wide range. For teaching vocabulary, the criterion should be range of usefulness and regularity, in the first stage. In the second stage, however, it should be range of usefulness alone. All the same frequency of occurrence should be the chief criterion for teaching vocabulary with a view to developing the four skills.

In recent years, words have been graded, listed and taught on the basis of frequency, that is, on the basis of the number of times they occur in the average reading material. Several scholars have made attempts to select a minimum of vocabulary by means of word counts and word frequency lists. The words that are most frequently used are considered to be the commonest words, and they are included in the necessary minimum vocabulary. We have thus some of the word frequency lists prepared by experts right from the early twenties.

Vocabulary selection and control began with Thorndike's publication of his first *Teacher's Word Book* in 1921. His aim was to make reading easier for American students by enabling them to acquire a wide reading vocabulary. In the material he selected, he established the frequency of the commonest 5000 words. In 1931 he published yet another frequency list entitled *The Teacher's WordBook of 20000 Words*. This was followed by the *Carnegie Report on Vocabulary Selection and Control* published in 1936 by Thorndike, Faucett, West and Palmer. Later in 1941 Thordike and Lorge brought out *The Teacher's Word Book of 30000 Words*. These studies have led Michael West to prepare *A General Service List of English Words* in 1950. This list defines the vocabulary of simplified English at the 2000-word level.

These frequency lists are useful in that when textbooks for students are prepared, emphasis can be laid on the study of the commonest 2000 words in the language in a properly graded manner. Also, the lists establish the fact that the minimum productive vocabulary for the student to write or speak fluently and comfortably on non-specialised subjects is to be somewhere in the 1500-2000 word range. The teaching of this vocabulary with the help of specially prepared textbooks should be one of the chief aims of the English teacher. Once this is done a greater mastery of the language and command of vocabulary can be achieved by the student on his own in course of time. As J.A. Bright and G.P. McGregor point out, "...if this active vocabulary is a good foundation for reading unsimplified English, he will go on learning new words for himself, and the natural process of movement at need from receptive to productive use can be allowed to take place unforced, and as far as the student is concerned almost unperceived."[4]

The textbooks that are intended for students should be readable; a text containing too many new words is unreadable. The new words that they have to study should be from within the 2000-word list. A few words from outside the list may be there in the text; if they are not too many no great difficulty will arise for the teacher and his students to plough through the text. Experience shows that more than 25 new words per thousand running words usually make a text difficult.

We have noted that direct teaching of vocabulary is out of the question and that teaching has to be contextualised. But how should we proceed to do this? The practice of vocabulary being taught by translation—i.e. each word being given its equivalent or non-equivalent in the first language has been found to be unsound. One reason for this is that exact equivalents are very often hard to find. Another reason is that a translation approach ignores the cultural and idiomatic aspects of the collocation of words. A third reason is that this approach reduces vocabulary teaching to the mere teaching of meaning. Actually, putting across the meaning is only a small part of vocabulary teaching. What is important is to teach students to use words meaningfully in their own sentences. That is to say, they should have a great deal of practice so as to have fluency in using them in speech and writing as well as an ability to understand them when they listen to others using them.

Vocabulary, both receptive and productive, will improve, if we actually train the students in the use of words. Ability to recognise the word is the first step. This depends on the student's hearing the word in isolation as well as in a sentence, and later in his pronouncing it. At this stage he need not know the meaning of the word. But the meaning should be explained to him in simple English, translation should be resorted to only as a last step. Apart from explanation, there are other ways by which the meaning of a new word can be taught to the class. The students may be asked to decipher the meaning from the context in which the word occurs. The teacher may himself use the word in sentences of his own describing familiar situations. Synonyms are also useful for teaching meaning. Having put across the meaning of a new word, the teacher should lead the students to practise the use of the words in their own sentences, both as an oral and a written exercise.

One of the main tasks of the teacher is to encourage the students at all times to learn new words and their use. Towards this end, they should be either provided with or be asked to provide themselves with personal dictionaries. A good dictionary that can be recommended to the class is *The Advanced Learner's Dictionary of Current English.* The class should also be given special training in the use of a dictionary and in gleaning such information as can be obtained from it about a word. The students should be made to realise that besides spelling, pronunciation, stress, and meaning or meanings, the dictionary gives us grammatical information and illustrative sentences as well.

While teaching vocabulary the teacher should pay special attention to the grammatical category to which a word belongs in the context and should make use of this as a starting point for teaching the uses of the word in other contexts in different levels of meaning. Grammatical information such as the absence of a plural form for the word (e.g. 'furniture') or the occurrence of a plural form that does not mean the same as what it means in the singular (e.g. 'damage') or how a word changes its meaning, and sometimes even category, with a change in pronunciation (e.g. 'invalid') should be taught. A change in the meaning of the word that occurs, when used in collocation with other words or idiomatic phrases in which it is the key word, may be explained with illustrative sentences. While explaining the meanings of adjectives such as 'historic', 'economic', 'credulous', etc., they may be distinguished from 'historical', 'economical', 'credible', etc. When a new verb is taught, the tense-form of the verb should also be taught. This is important because irregular verbs generally pose difficulties to students.

There are many ways by which a student can build up a sizable vocabulary; so too, there are many approaches to the teaching of vocabulary. The principle to be stressed, however, is the value of learning as many words as possible, without restricting them either to those in the lessons or to those in some particular list. In teaching vocabulary the main objective of learning a language—mastering it as a living, usable language for all forms of communication—must always be kept in mind. If too much stress is placed on the difference between active and passive vocabulary, the student's incentive to increase his vocabulary will suffer a setback. Each student requires the largest possible vocabulary to express himself to his satisfaction, and nothing should act as a disincentive to his effort to develop a good vocabulary. Every possible device should be used to encourage the student in building up his vocabulary—by means of synonyms, antonyms and onomatopoeic words as well as by guessing at meanings from contexts, studying prefixes and suffixes and analysing words. The teacher who uses the second language in class constantly and does not use the first language of his students helps them acquire a good vocabulary. Though this may be largely a passive vocabulary, at first retained by ear and not always too accurately retained, yet eventually it becomes part of their active vocabulary without their realising it.

References

1.   Allen, Harold B (ed.), *Teaching English as a Second Language,* p. 213
2.   Lado, Robert, *Language Teaching,* p. 117
3.   Quoted on p. 209 in *Teaching English as a Second Language,* edited by Harold B. Allen
4.   Bright, J.A. & McGregor, G.P., *Teaching English as a Second Language,* p. 19.

For Further Reading

1.   Fries, C.C., *The Structure of English,* Longman, 1957
2.   Morris, 1., *The Art of Teaching English as a Living Language,* Macmillan, 1955
3.   Osman, N., *Word Function and Dictionary Use, Oxford University Press,* 1965

TEN

CLASSROOM PROCEDURES

One of the fundamental principles of all effective teaching is that a teacher should plan and prepare his lesson beforehand. No teaching should be casual and careless. A casual approach on the part of the teacher results in sheer waste of time and does not make any contribution to the learning process. Whether it be the teaching of the text, grammar, pronunciation or vocabulary or the four skills or even the handling of a tutorial class, the teacher should not face his students without adequate planning and preparation.

What is meant by planning and preparation? Planning involves questions like what to teach and how to put across to the students what one intends to teach them. If the teacher decides on teaching a prose text, then care should be bestowed on the selection of the text so that the students do not find it too difficult. (Perhaps selection does not pose much of a problem for the Indian teacher of English as the textbook he has to teach at a particular level has been selected and prescribed by the Board of Studies. But here too, the teacher has a role: he may grade the lessons or essays in the textbook and start teaching the simpler ones first.)

The criteria of selection are mainly suitability and structural and verbal simplicity. Suitability means that the passage selected is the right one for the class. A passage that is too difficult for the class to follow will not serve any useful purpose. The passage should not contain far too many difficult words and far too many complicated structures. The presence of too many difficult words and difficult structures will militate against the students' taking an interest in the passage. The subject matter of the passage should also be interesting enough for the students.

Once selection of the prose text is made, the teacher has to decide on the procedure to follow in the class. He may decide on asking the students to read silently in class a fixed portion of the text within a specified time or on reading out that portion himself to the class. The next step for him is to frame a few questions which he is to ask the students to test their comprehension. The third step is to explain the passage. While explaining, the teacher has to bear in mind the difficulties of the students as revealed in their answers to the questions earlier asked. Finally, as an essential part of planning, he should decide on the items he is going to teach with the help of the text. Vocabulary and structures are important items.

Having thus planned the procedure to be adopted, the teacher should prepare himself thoroughly for imparting instruction. First and foremost, he should read the text closely and clear his own doubts as to the exact meanings of words and phrases, the significance of references and allusions, etc. Next he should frame the questions that he is going to ask the class, besides picking out the words, structures, etc. requiring explanation; he should also be ready with model sentences illustrating the use of those words and structures which he wants his students to learn by their own use.

The method of teaching a prose text that is generally adopted by teachers in Indian colleges is unsound. What they do is to read out rapidly the text in class and offer explanations of words and sentences in a haphazard manner (sometimes in the mother tongue of the students), and dictate notes which are taken down incorrectly by the students. This kind of teaching is a one-sided performance, and is at its best a 'monologue'. As we have noted elsewhere in the book, lecturing does not teach. The ideal thing for the teacher to do is to help the students understand the passage as best they themselves can. The procedure suggested above will be of help inasmuch as the students are asked to read the text silently on their own or to read it with the teacher and then to answer the comprehension questions put to them by the teacher; in other words, the method ensures interaction between the teacher and the taught, besides better student activity.

Poetry can also be similarly taught, though a slightly different procedure may have to be followed. The teacher may read the poem aloud in class with appropriate stress and intonation. (While teaching poetry the students' attention may be drawn to stress, intonation, rhythm, rhyme, etc.) A theme-based approach is found to be effective. The teacher should, therefore, have a lesson plan with a number of questions that will lead the students to the theme of the poem and to the devices used by the poet to deal with the theme. Consider, for instance, the poem, "A River" by A.K. Ramanujan:

In Madurai,
city of temples and poets
who sang of cities and temples:
every summer

a river dries to a trickle
in the sand,
bearing the sand-ribs
straw and women's hair
clogging the watergates
at the rusty bars
under the bridges with patches
of repair all over them,
the wet stones glistening like sleepy
crocodiles, the dry ones
shaven water-buffaloes lounging in the sun.

The poets sang only of the floods.

He was there for a day
when they had the floods.
People everywhere talked
of the inches rising,
of the precise number of cobbled steps
run over by water, rising
on the bathing places,
and the way it carried off three village houses,
one pregnant woman
and a couple of cows
named Gopi and Brinda, as usual.

The new poets still quoted
the old poets, but no one spoke
in verse
of the pregnant woman
drowned, with perhaps twins in her,
kicking at blank walls
even before birth.

He said:
the river has water enough
to be poetic
about only once a year
and then
it carries away

in the first half-hour
three village houses,
a couple of cows
named Gopi and Brinda
and one pregnant woman
expecting identical twins
with no moles on their bodies,
with different-coloured diapers

to tell them apart.

The following is a lesson plan based on the poem:
1. Introduce the poem to the class. Some personal details of the poet
    may be given to the class. Tell the class that the river is the Vakai
    flowing through the historical city of Madurai.
2. Read out the poem to the class once
3. Ask the students to make a note of the words and phrases that they
    do not know. Explain these words and phrases; if notes are provided
    at the end, ask the students to consult them.
4. Read out the poem once again and ask the following questions:
    (a) What happens to the river every summer?
    (b) How does the poet describe the river?
    (c) What is the significance of the crocodile and buffalo images?
    (d) Who is 'He' in the poem? A choric voice or the poet himself?
    (e) What did 'He' hear people talk when they had floods?
    (f) What did no one speak of?
    (g) What did 'He' say?
    (h) How is 'His' second account different from the first?
5. Read out the poem a third time and draw the students' attention to
    the following sets of lines and ask the questions based on each set:

    (a) the wet stones glistening like sleepy
         crocodiles, the dry ones
         shaven water-buffaloes lounging in the sun.
    (i) Explain the reason for the use of these images.
    (ii) What is the point of comparison between the wet stones and the
         sleepy crocodiles?
    (iii) Why are the dry stones compared to water buffaloes?
    (b) People everywhere talked
         of the inches rising,

of the precise number of cobbled steps
run over by the water, rising
on the bathing places
..... as usual,
(i) Who quoted the words of the people?
(ii) What is the significance of the mention of the pregnant woman?
(iii) Why are the cows mentioned and named?
(c) The new poets still quoted
the old poets, but no one spoke
in verse
of the pregnant woman
........before birth.
(i) Why did the new poets still quote the old ones?
(ii) What is the implication of the statement that no one spoke in verse of the pregnant woman?
(iii) Why did the twins kick at blank walls even before birth?
6.   Explain to the class the stylistic features of the poem.
7.   Sum up the poem to the class.

The reason why teaching English poetry in the second language situation is not successful is that the poems selected are often difficult and express experience and sensibility that are unfamiliar to our students, and that the teacher, more often than not, resorts to paraphrasing and translation for teaching the poems. Careful selection of poems and a planned, well-prepared approach can be a remedy. When poems are selected, it should be ensured that they do not present too many linguistic difficulties to the class and that they deal with themes of universal interest.

Planning and preparation on the part of the teacher are absolutely necessary when he teaches a novel, a short story or a drama. (A full-length novel, short story or drama is good material for language teaching. But here too, much depends on selection. The novel or short story should be simple enough or it should be a simplified version of the original; the dialogue in the novel, short story, or drama selected for students' use should be free from regional dialects.) As part of his preparation for the teaching of a novel or a play, the teacher should read it from beginning to end thoroughly and critically. His reading of the work should not be piecemeal. That is to say, he should not begin teaching a novel or a play without having gone through it fully. Reading the text in full alone will enable him to plan his lessons; if fully acquainted with the text of the novel or the play, he will be able to divide it into units and topics, and plan his classroom work, both linguistic and literary, on the basis of these units and topics.

While planning lessons based on a novel or a play, the teacher should first of all pay attention to its content and theme, and then only to language exercises. The students' familiarity with the theme and content of the novel or the play and with the culture and life of the people dealt with in the work will make them learn the language easily and effectively.

Some of the teachers entertain the notion that teaching grammar and composition does not call for planning and preparation. They believe that since they know the grammar of the language, it is enough if they explain the grammatical item to the students and set them an exercise; so too they think that a composition class can be handled casually as their task is only to set an exercise, and it is for the students to write it.

These notions of the teacher are erroneous. He knows the grammar all right, there may be a prescribed grammar textbook too for him to follow. Even then, planning and preparation are necessary in so far as he has to make the teaching interesting and the class alive, alert and attentive as well as responsive to what is being done. Moreover, without planning and preparation the teacher will be at a loss to decide on the appropriate grammatical item to be taught in a particular class and on how to put it across most effectively to the students. The teacher has to decide on the grammatical item appropriate to the standard and achievement of the class; he has also to decide on the best possible approach to introduce the item. That is to say, whether or not the grammatical item should be introduced to the class by definition or through illustrations and examples has to be decided by him beforehand. Suppose he decides on teaching the articles; he may choose to introduce the articles by definitions or he may ask the students to read a suitable passage and ask them to pick out 'the' and 'a' or 'an' in it and then proceed to indicate the function of 'the' and 'a' or 'an' in every instance as a starting point before teaching them the different uses of the articles.

While teaching a grammatical item too, a lesson plan is useful, and makes teaching more effective. The following lesson plan for the teaching of the articles is an example:

1. Introduce the articles. The students are asked to pick out 'the', and 'a' or 'an' in a given passage.
2. Explain the functions of 'the' and 'a' or 'an'. Students are asked to illustrate.
3. The main uses of 'a' or 'an'. Attention should be drawn to 'year' and 'ear' as well as words beginning with long 'u' and short 'u' and

the confusion in the use of 'a' or 'an'. Students are asked to give examples.

4. The main uses of 'the'. Attention should be drawn to phrases such as 'to the pictures', 'to the races', 'to the hills', etc.
5. Explain why 'the' is omitted in phrases such as 'on earth', 'by land', 'at sea', etc. Students are asked to give examples.
6. Explain how 'to the bed', 'to the school', 'to the church', etc. are different from 'to bed', 'to school', 'to church', etc.
7. The use of 'the' before an adjective. Give illustrative sentences and ask the students to make their own sentences.
8. The use of 'the' before a singular noun to denote a class or species. Examples.
9. The distinction between 'most important' and 'the most important'. Examples.

Composition or tutorial work in class also requires planning and preparation on the part of the teacher, for the planning and spadework. done beforehand by the teacher enable him to guide the students to the task. Suppose the task is paragraph writing; it is not enough that the teacher asks the students to write a paragraph on a topic and then sit back in his chair. He should have planned his work and have prepared himself to introduce the students to paragraph writing. Perhaps it is necessary for him to teach them first of all the essential elements of a paragraph and how to construct a good paragraph with a topic sentence that expresses the central idea. Then, while assigning the task he should guide the students to the writing of the paragraph on a given topic.

A similar approach is useful for the teaching of essay-writing too. But again, before assigning the task of writing an essay on a topic, the students should be taught the mechanics of writing an essay. A lesson plan such as the following will be helpful:

1. What is an essay?
2. Characteristics of a good essay?
    (a) unity
    (b) balance
    (c) coherence
    (d) length
    (e) emphasis.
3. Stages of essay-writing:
    (a) analysing the topic
    (b) organising the material
    (c) preparing the outline

4.	Points to be borne in mind for writing well.

In the first stage of essay-writing it is advisable for the teacher to guide the students by discussing with them the points that may be developed in the essay and by helping them in the preparation of the outline. Suppose the topic assigned to the students is: "Advertising: Its Uses and Abuses". The teacher may start off with a discussion; the students should be encouraged to join in the discussion. At the end of the discussion the teacher may help them in drawing up an outline of the essay as given below:

1.	Introduction
2.	The purpose of advertising
3.	The positive role of advertising
4.	Main objective—promotion of sales
5.	Advertising agencies—their role
6.	The range of the media
7.	Advertising—its abuses
8.	Conclusion.

Apart from planning, preparation and effective classroom work, the teacher should follow up his teaching with remedial work. This is because no student can be expected to absorb and retain fully and perfectly what has been taught. Errors are always made by him, and these demand remedial work, especially when these errors constitute violation of the normal rules of the language. In a second language situation the errors arise mainly from (a) mother tongue interference, (b) false analogy, and (c) sheer muddle.

How should the teacher set about his task of remedial work? He should first of all establish what the error is. Once this is done, he should track it down to its source. If it is due to mother tongue interference, the teacher should attempt a little contrastive analysis (i.e. comparing the learner's mother tongue with the target language). Also, in his remedial teaching he should give priority to those mistakes that are more serious. Mistakes in the overall structure of sentences, tense, concord, case, articles, etc., are generally regarded as serious.

The success of remedial work depends on careful correction of written work, and error analysis. While correcting the exercises of his students, the teacher should mark mistakes using symbols so that the students themselves can be made to correct them later. It is advisable that the students write out all corrections in full and that the teacher goes through them.

Error analysis may be done coarsely. Ten classified categories—spelling, punctuation, verb form, tense, preposition, pronoun, word order, concord, articles, and vocabulary—are enough. But they should be dealt with one after the other, and not all at the same time.

The extra time given to full correction and analysis may be compensated for by setting shorter assignments. It is far better for the students to write short pieces carefully and have them thoroughly corrected and usefully analysed than to write long pieces carelessly and have them superficially scrutinised. All experience shows that the lightening of the burden on the teacher through the improvement in the work submitted soon makes up for the extra burden imposed at first by error analysis.

The substitution table is an invaluable device for remedial drilling in both speech and writing. An excellent set of substitution tables, with an unusually well-chosen vocabulary is provided by H.V. George in his *Substitution Tables for Students of English* (Cambridge University Press).

For Further Reading

Close, R.A., *A University Grammar of English Workbook,* Longman, 1974
Dodd, W.A., *The Teacher at Work,* Oxford University Press, 1970
Jupp, T.C. and Milne, J., *Guided Course in English Composition,* Heinemann, 1968
__________, *Guided Paragraph Writing,* Heinemann, 1972
Richards, J.C. (ed.), *Error Analysis,* Longman, 1974

ELEVEN

METHODS OF EVALUATION

If teaching and learning are to go on efficiently, the achievement of students needs to be constantly measured. That is to say, a good deal of time and attention should be devoted to the assessment of the progress made by the students. It is in this connection that evaluation in any scheme of teaching becomes important.

Evaluation serves some useful purposes. These may be listed as follows:

(a) assessment of attainment, for purposes of awarding a qualification or for selection and placement;

(b) prediction of future progress;

(c) measurement of the value of teaching methods and procedures —an essential part of the design of experiments in teaching;

(d) diagnosis of individual or group difficulties;

(e) measurement of aptitude.

Evaluation, in other words, aims at ascertaining aptitude, proficiency and achievement and at performing a diagnosis of difficulties for future action. Evaluation is carried out by means of tests and examinations. The words, 'test' and 'examination', overlap in their meanings. 'Examination' is the term favoured when promotion or qualification for a career is in question or when it is a formal set-piece kind of assessment. It usually consists of two-hour or three-hour papers which students have to work for themselves without any access to the textbooks, notes or dictionaries and without any guidance from teacher or fellow-students. In India examinations are conducted by Boards, Directorates and Universities as well as by Departments in autonomous colleges.

A good examination has two characteristics. It conforms very closely to the declared objectives of the course (which must be valuable and attainable). It does justice between candidate and candidate. The second characteristic which demands justice and fairplay makes objectivity an imperative necessity, though objectivity in paper-setting and valuation is not easy to attain fully, and no two paper-setters are likely to place the same weight of emphasis on the same categories of linguistic performance.

The word 'test' covers an immense range of evaluation procedures, from a quick quiz or a piece of home-work to a qualifying examination. It is very often a teacher-devised activity carried out in the classroom and used by the teacher for assessing the day-to-day progress of his students. It may be more or less formal or more or less carefully prepared. Testing has three objectives. It aims at evaluating the student's performance from time to time so that appropriate remedial steps can be taken to bring him up to the expected standard. It enables the teacher to know in time whether or not the course objectives are being fulfilled. It puts the student wise in time as to his own achievement or non-achievement.

Objectivity is highly desirable in both examinations and tests. In order to achieve objectivity in assessment and evaluation, tests that can be marked almost entirely mechanically by any careful and honest person, from the paper-setter to a clerk, are devised. The tests so devised are known as objective tests.

The guidelines given below are intended to ensure objectivity in tests and examinations:

(a) Objectivity is enhanced and discrepancies are reduced when, as far as possible, only one skill is tested and marked at a time. (This is why precis-writing of the conventional type as an examination item is frowned upon. In precis-writing it is not only comprehension but also composition that is tested as students are asked to summarise the passage in their own words reducing it to one-third of its original length).

(b) Multiple-choice questions are particularly valuable for testing the receptive skills because no composition skill is required in the answering. The following question is taken from a reading-comprehension test which proved a searching one for foreign post-graduate students in Britain:-

Question: If the statement in italics given below is true, one and only one of the four statements below it must be true. Write a bold cross right over the number at the bottom of the correct statement

"Mars is the only planet in the solar system of which the surface can be directly observed by means of optical instruments."

(1) The surface of Mars can be studied only by means of a telescope.

(2) Optical instruments are useless for the study of any planet in the solar system other than Mars.

(3) All planets in orbit around the sun, except for Mars, have their surfaces obscured from observation from the earth by some kind of non-transparent environment.

(4) Mars differs from all other planets in the solar system in respect of the fact that it has no atmosphere to prevent its surface from being directly viewed through optical instruments.

(1)   (2)   (3)   (4)

The above specimen shows that an objectively scored test item need not be childishly simple. There is, however, a possibility that objective tests become vitiated, if guesswork helps the student in arriving at the right answer.

(c) In a four-choice question there is a twenty-five per cent chance that the right answer will be given by a person who is ignorant of the subject and merely guessing. Hence, for examining purposes, multiple-choice questions must be set in large numbers.

(d) If, however, the choice range is increased to five, fewer questions need be set, but five-choice questions are harder to compose. If the choice rate is decreased to three, more questions must be set, but they will be easier to compose.

(c) A good deal of sophistication and diligence is required to compose multiple-choice questions. They are laborious to construct, but nearly all the labour is taken out of marking. Hence, they are particularly attractive when large numbers of students are to be tested.

(f) Well-constructed objectively scored tests are probably the finest instrument we have for testing, listening and reading. They can be made very searching, and offer very safe measurements of true performance.

The teacher of English as a second language should have training and practice in designing both objective and non-objective tests. These tests should enable him to measure his students' achievement. He should, however, have his objectives well-defined. The validity of his tests depends on these objectives. Validity is obtained only when the teacher is sure in his own mind as to the skills and abilities which he sets out to measure. The question which the teacher has to ask himself while devising a test is: "Does it work?". It should work in four ways. It should be a reliable measure. A test is reliable if it gives the same results under the same conditions. It is like any measuring instrument, say a thermometer. It should not give different readings when the temperature is the same. The causes of unreliability are vague and ambiguous questions, questions which can be answered by a process of elimination, questions which cover only a small sample of skills or knowledge involved and questions which admit of different answers and of subjective evaluation by the teacher. Reliability is higher in objective tests than in non-objective tests.

The second way the test should work is that it should enable the teacher to distinguish between one student and another and arrive at an assessment of each one. The third way it should work depends upon its adequacy; it should be adequate to measure what it is supposed to measure. The fourth way the test should work concerns its practicability. The test should be practicable; by practicability is meant the extent to which the test is readily usable and is eventually useful to the process of teaching and learning.

In India classroom tests are not regularly and systematically conducted. No sincere effort is made to assess the students' achievement from time to time. This neglect has led to undue importance being given to examinations conducted by the Boards or Universities. These examinations determine at best only the achievement of students for purposes of rating them on the basis of their marks. The teaching of English in our educational institutions should pay special attention to periodic tests aimed at assessing their achievement with a view to knowing their standard as well as their weaknesses so that remedial measures can be taken in time to improve their standard and bring it up to the expected terminal behaviour.

The tests or examinations that we at present conduct do not take into account all the linguistic aspects that are to be tested. Our emphasis in these tests is mainly on the students' ability to express facts, ideas or thoughts in writing. So, our tests are not linguistically sound. The tests are, to that extent not valid and do not serve as a measure of the students' achievement or as a means to know their difficulties. The fact is that most of our teachers do not have the know-how for setting question papers for tests that will measure their students' achievement in the four skills.

In the classroom the teacher should conduct achievement rather than proficiency and prognostic tests. Achievement tests are intended to measure success in a particular sequence of learning whereas prognostic tests are intended to predict how successful the student is likely to be (on the basis of his aptitude). Proficiency tests are those that measure the students' standard or skill irrespective of training. These tests—prognostic and proficiency—are useful as entrance tests to assess the entry behaviour of students at the commencement of a course.

In the achievement tests designed by the teacher he should take into account the distinctive nature of the four-language skills and test them separately. The tests we use at present test the writing aspect mainly, and the reading aspect partly. Listening comprehension (auditory discrimination of phonemes, allophones and suprasegmentals) and speaking (oral production of phonemes, allophones and suprasegmenas) as skills are neglected. Our emphasis in tests is on knowledge of structure, vocabulary and idiomatic phrases. Our achievement tests are, therefore, inadequate and deficient.

Yet another reason why our achievement tests are inadequate is that we do not take into consideration the student's mother tongue while preparing our tests. The tests will be much more effective if we base the test items on the points of difficulty experienced by the student as a result of interference from his mother tongue. A contrastive analysis of the mother tongue and English will reveal these points of difficulty to the teacher.

While preparing the tests, the teacher should know his goals and reduce them to their simplest elements and know what ability he is testing. Besides, he should test one ability at a time. Separate tests for listening comprehension, speaking ability, reading comprehension and writing ability should be set. Questions should be framed in such a way that guessing on the part of students should not lead them to the right answers; nor should the questions be vague or ambiguous.

Achievement tests may be oral or written. The conventional non-objective type of oral test often consists of a passage to be read aloud, followed by questions about its content. This enables the teacher to test the student's pronunciation as well as his comprehension. Yet, such a test is unsatisfactory because it is time-consuming and because too many different aspects—sounds, stress, rhythm, intonation, fluency as well as comprehension—are tested simultaneously. This type of test can be streamlined if one aspect at a time is judged on the basis of multiple-choice questions given in writing along with the passage to the students. This will also effect a kind of standardisation and bring in a measure of objectivity. The non-objectivity of oral examinations may also be reduced by recording the students' answers for replay and assessment by the teacher later.

Written tests may aim at the assessment of not only graphic skills but also to some extent of audio-lingual skills. Objective written tests have the advantage of pin-pointing problems of learning. Dictation, for example, may test both graphic and audio-lingual skills. The students' control of English grammar must be tested in use, and this can best be achieved by objective tests which select and isolate grammatical features causing difficulty in particular areas. No knowledge of any grammatical terminology need be demanded from the students.

In the early stages of learning continuous writing can be tested objectively by assessing certain factors in isolation. Essay-writing should not be tried in the early stages; it is not an appropriate test at all levels. Essay-writing should, however, be a test at a higher stage.

In conclusion we may say that no teaching of English as a second-language is effective without periodic tests being held to test the four skills. The teacher on his part should make use of the results of the tests for future guidance in imparting instruction to the students. What is practicable for him is to have a system of tests which at the very elementary stage will be almost entirely objective and at the advanced stage almost entirely non-objective with both types existing side by side in the intervening stages.

For Further Reading

1. Harris, D.P., *Testing English as a Second Language,* New York: McGraw-Hill, 1969
2. Lado, R., *English Language Test for Foreign Students,* Ann Arbor: Wahr, 1960
3. Valette, R.M., *Modern Language Testing: A Handbook,* New York: Harcourt Brace, 1967

TWELVE

THE USE OF AUDIO-VISUAL AIDS

No effective teaching is possible without appropriate aids. This is perhaps more true of teaching a second-language than of teaching one's own mother tongue or a subject. These aids are visual, audio or audio-visual. Visual aids help the students see and comprehend what they are taught whereas audio-aids help them learn from what they hear. Audio-visual aids combine in themselves the technology of teaching through hearing and seeing.

The most versatile and indispensable visual aid is the blackboard. No classroom can be without a blackboard. Though teachers make use of the blackboard for language lessons, yet there is no blackboard method of teaching a second-language. However, the use of the blackboard in the classroom for teaching should be deliberately planned and systematically implemented. What is meant is that the teacher, instead of writing: haphazardly on the blackboard, should use it for drawing the students' attention to the main points of the lesson, and those alone, in a systematic manner as the lesson is in progress. So, at the beginning of a lesson any writing on the blackboard, which is not relevant to the lesson, should be wiped off, and in its place, what is going to be taught should be written. This is important because any material on the board that has no relation to the lesson will be a source of distraction to the students. Spellings of words and their pronunciations can be taught fairly effectively, when they are written on the blackboard; the pronunciation should be written in the phonetic script. Coloured chalk can be used for distinguishing between spellings or between sounds which pose problems for the students. The blackboard should not be used for writing more than a word or a sentence at a time; for such haphazard writing, while the lesson is in progress, is likely to distract the students' attention. If, however, it is necessary to present any lengthy material on the board, it should be written on it before the commencement of the lesson. In a dictation class the blackboard is of great use; the material for dictation can be written on the side of the board that is not visible to the students, earlier or at the time of dictation, by a student or the teacher himself, and when the dictation is over, what is written on the board can be put in full view of the students for them to correct on their own the mistakes they have made while taking down the dictation.

Flash cards and charts are useful visual aids. Flash cards are sets of cards with words or phrases written on one side and their meanings on the other. The students can look up the word or phrase and later check their response against the back of the cards. For pronunciation practice flash cards with words on one side and their phonetic transcriptions on the other side are useful. Similarly, spellings too can be taught with the help of flash cards.

There are different kinds of charts available for teaching sentence patterns as well as the phonetic script. A chart displaying the international phonetic script may be hung permanently in the classrooms. A chart for pattern practice has pictures and sentences such as 'It's a boy', 'It's an orange', etc., describing the pictures. The teacher can read out each sentence, and ask the class to repeat it. The same chart can be used by the teacher for putting questions and eliciting affirmative and negative short answers based on the pictures.

Slides and slide projectors, film strips, opaque projectors or epidiascopes and overhead projectors are some other visual aids. These visual aids are useful for making a lesson vivid and clear. Slides and slide projectors can be used for showing cultural objects in full colour and providing the stimulus for controlled speaking practice or free conversation. Film strips can similarly be used for training in informal conversation under the guidance of the teacher. The opaque projector or epidiascope is useful for projecting images of both opaque and transparent objects. The teacher may use it for reflecting any page in a book or a sheet on a screen in any darkened room. The opaque projector has the additional advantage over slide projectors in that any material can be shown as it is with its help.

The use of the overhead projector results in the projection of what the teacher writes on a transparent plastic film on to a screen behind him as he faces the class. This has an advantage over the blackboard in that the teacher does not have to turn his back to the class to write on the board. The use of overhead projectors is confined to the projection of illustrated drawings and notes. This is because integrated graded language materials for use through overhead projectors have not been developed. One of the practical applications of the overhead projector is during a dictation period when the teacher can have the students correct their own papers through the projection of the material on the screen at the appropriate moment.

The gramophone and the tape recorder come in handy as audio-aids. These can be used for playing records of fables, stories, plays, poems, etc., to the class. A portion of the recorded text may be played and necessary explanations given by the teacher. The text in full may be played again; simultaneously a detailed analysis of the text followed by questions put by the teacher to individual students may be attempted.

The tape-recorder has advantages over the gramophone. This is because the former can be used for present recording and replaying, and the tape thus recorded can be used indefinitely, if the recording is meant to be permanent. If, however, the recording is not meant to be permanent, it can be erased by recording again on top of it. Permanent recordings varying from a few minutes to several hours can be made on the tape and retained for later use.

One of the important uses of the tape-recorder in the classroom is that it enables the students to hear their own voices. It would be quite a thrilling experience for them. Moreover, the tape recorder can be used for class oral work leading to the elimination of personal faults in pronunciation, intonation and rhythm. It may, however, be borne in mind that any remedial work in pronunciation, intonation etc., will have better results, if it is done in small groups rather than in a large class. S.R. Ingram in his paper on audio-aids in modern language teaching suggests the following technique of using the tape recorder with young beginners: "Choose your material carefully—say two sentences illustrating certain points of pronunciation or intonation. Practise them with a small number of pupils before you record—this to give them confidence as well as practice—then record their voices straight off. Play the recording back straight through and let the whole group hear the accurate record of what took place. Either let the group criticise or do so yourself, stopping the machine at appropriate points. The same reading can be used several times to illustrate different points and the interest can thus be maintained quite a long time, as the participants are both present and known to the rest of the group. Next re-record, hoping you have improved on the original, and of course, using the same speakers. Finally, play the original and the second recording and try to learn from it all."[1]

There is, however, nothing hard and fast about this technique; the teacher should adapt it to suit his needs. Experience tells us that most students readily develop an interest in this kind of work.

The tape recorder can also be used for dictation from the very elementary reproduction stage to the very advanced unseen test. The passage for dictation may be recorded beforehand, with repetitions and pauses. In the classroom the record is played for the students to take down. Their first effort may be full of mistakes; they will show improvement on their second and third attempts. The practice in listening to the recorded material is also training in listening comprehension.

Poetry can be taught with the help of a tape recorder with ease and delight. The record of a poem can be played and replayed; hearing the poem again and again, especially when it is a professional version, is to get at its beauties and meaning gradually. The students will learn to read a poem well only if they hear it well read or said. The professional rendering of a poem played by the tape recorder will enable the students to appreciate the importance of sound, inflection, stress, pause, intonation, etc, in poetry.

According to Ingram this technique of teaching poetry with the help of a tape recorder has many possible variations. He says: "There is no one correct and definitive interpretation of a poem. It is best therefore to make a clear and obvious decision as to what is important and try to stick to it, The rhythm must be clearly defined, pauses and stresses carefully marked. The teacher first of all reads the poem to the class, trying to give his very best performance... Any necessary explanation or commentary is then given, but usually translation as such is avoided, for a good delivery of the poem is better than any translation."[2]

The teacher's reading of the poem may be followed by a recording of the reading with students co-operating by keeping absolutely quiet. A discussion of the flaws of the reading may be allowed. A re-recording may be done so that the flaws, if any, may be eliminated. Some of the students may have their readings of the poem recorded and played back; the flaws in these readings may be discussed and criticized. Before the lesson ends, once again the teacher may himself recite the poem in full to the class.

The tape recorder can be a valuable aid in the teaching of drama too. Tapes of well-known plays are available and can be used to supplement classroom activity. The tape recorder can also be used for recording the dialogue of the play spoken by some students of the class who are assigned particular roles. What is recorded can be played back, and the flaws in their speaking the dialogue, with special emphasis on pronunciation, stress, intonation, etc. may be pointed out by the teacher. Once the flaws are more or less eliminated, a re-recording of the dialogue may be done and played back to the class. If portions of the play are selected and roles assigned to the students turn by turn, the entire class will get enough practice.

Much of the language learning depends on the practice of oral-aural skills. We have seen that the tape recorder is a convenient aid for the practice of these language skills. There is yet another aid called the language laboratory, which, if put to effective use, will provide the students with adequate opportunities to practise oral-aural language skills. Robert Lado points out that there are two conflicting views on the role of the language laboratory in the teaching of a language. The first view is that the language laboratory is "the centre of language teaching with the teacher assisting the lab operation and adjusting to it". The second is that it "is a teaching aid, with the class as the centre."[3] The first view is indefensible; for it relegates the teacher's role to that of a mechanic and a subordinate and assigns a superior role to the language laboratory and the ready-made materials which may be used independently by the students. In defence of "the lab-as-an-aid point of view", Lado sets forth the following arguments: "1. The teacher is clearly thought of as the central figure teaching the students. 2. The lab is one more aid, not the central component of teaching. 3. The lab materials are designed to supplement class work selectively. 4. The materials are not complete lessons.[4] The point is that the successful use of the language laboratory as an aid depends on the availability of teachers who know how to handle the equipment, employ the new techniques, and at the same time, conduct a class.

A language laboratory is a room in which the students are isolated from each other by soundproof walls. Each room has the necessary equipment for practice by the students. The advantages of the set-up are that each student can practise speaking without disturbing others and without being disturbed by others and that a whole class of students can simultaneously practise the oral-aural language skills.

Language laboratories range from those with quite simple equipment to those with complicated equipment. According to S. Pit Corder[5], it is better in the early stage to have simple equipment. He suggests three stages in the development of a laboratory. In the first stage there should be a number of soundproof booths, each fitted with a set of headphones connected to a microphone in front of the teacher. This arrangement enables the students to listen to the teacher and carry out his instructions, take down his dictation or answer his questions. Also, the teacher can speak direct to all students together and can play the recorded material for the benefit of all. The arrangement has, however, some drawbacks:

the teacher cannot check up on the students' work; he is out of sight of the students and does not have any means to know whether they are attentive or not.

The second stage is an improvement upon the first one in that the teacher has earphones that are connected with a microphone in each student's booth in addition to the facilities mentioned above. In this stage individual students can speak to the teacher who can monitor their performance and speak to any student individually.

A further development in the third stage consists in the introduction of a tape recorder into each student's booth. So, in addition to the facilities available in the earlier two stages of development, in this stage the students can record the teacher's and their own voices on their tape recorders and play back the results and make comparisons. The teacher can also monitor the work of each one of the students. Special dual-track tape recorders may be introduced in this stage so that the teacher's model can be played and the student's copy recorded, all in one operation.

Now that television has come into vogue, it has become a key audio-visual aid today. For the teaching of English as a second-language in India, it can be of great help. Some of the uses of television are: through it the services of a good teacher can be made available to a large number of students at the same time; video-recordings of good lessons can be put to effective use in educational institutions through T.V. sets fitted with video cassette projectors; national and regional telecasts of English lessons can be attended by the students; films based on literary classics can be seen and practise in listening comprehension gained.

The cost of T.V. sets need not frighten the educational authorities; for the cost of teaching English through television on a large scale is relatively small compared with providing qualified teachers. This does not, however, mean that television is the answer to the inadequacies of teaching English as a second-language. The point is that television can play an increasingly significant role in the solution to our problem of overcoming most of the inadequacies with which we are confronted, provided teaching through television is done by skilful, inspired teachers, backed by sound advice from linguists and producers of video cassettes.

As already mentioned, a significant use of television lies in the fact that educational films based on literary classics, now available in cassettes, can be shown through it. These films will bring to the classroom a realism in the teaching of English that cannot otherwise be attained. Moreover, they serve as supplementary material to the teaching of the language in so far as the students get not only an opportunity to listen to

English being spoken in varying contexts and situations but also a taste of the culture of the people who use English as their first language.

The increasing use of audio-visual aids in second-language teaching is based on the modern audio-lingual theory which stresses a listening-speaking-reading-writing sequence in second-language learning situations. The theory insists that learning to speak a language becomes easier, if the learner has enough training comprehension. Linguists and language-teaching experts lay emphasis on planned listening experiences. Their main arguments are:

1. Ear-training facilitates speaking. Articulation is dependent upon hearing sounds accurately...

2. Concentration on one skill at a time facilitates learning by reducing the load on the student and by permitting the use of materials and techniques geared to the specific objectives and requirements of each skill.

3. When students are required to speak from the outset, the likelihood of errors is increased... Where listening comprehension precedes speaking, the student's initial experience includes more correct responses and more frequent positive reinforcement, less apprehension, and more rapid development of confidence in his language learning ability.

4. Prematurely listening to his own unauthenticated pronunciation, and to that of other students, may interfere with the student's discrimination and retention of correct sounds.[6]

No audio-lingual approach can, however, be successful in the absence of qualified, trained teachers. Machines cannot replace teachers. The approach is and ought to be teacher-centred; that is to say, the aids require planned utilization by specially trained teachers. The high incidence of poorly qualified teachers only increases the waste of student time and public resources. Good teachers, good textbooks, records, tapes, tape recorders, language laboratories, television sets, cassettes and other audio-visual aids are an indispensable condition for a successful implementation of any scheme of teaching English as a second language in India.

References

1. Allen, H.B., (Ed.), *Teaching English as a Second Language*, pp. 349-50, "Audio-Aids in Modern Language Teaching" by S.R. Ingram.
2. ibid., 350

3.   Lado, Robert, *Language Teaching: A Scientific Approach,* p. 173
4.   ibid., p. 174
5.   Allen, H.B., (Ed.), *Teaching English as a Second Language,* pp. 343-44, "The Language Laboratory" by S. Pit Corder
6.   ibid., p. 353, "Emphasizing the Audio in the Audio-Lingual Approach" by Gerald Newmark and Edward Diller

For Further Reading

1.   Lee, W.R., *Simple Audio-Visual Aids to Foreign Language Teaching,* London: O.U.P., 1965
2.   Allen, H.B., (Ed.), *Teaching English as a Second Language,* Bombay: Tata McGraw-Hill Publishing Co. Ltd., 1965, pp. 341-61
3.   Lado, Robert, *Language Teaching: A Scientific Approach,* Bombay: Tata McGraw-Hill Publishing Co. Ltd., pp. 173-204

THIRTEEN

LITERATURE AND SECOND-LANGUAGE LEARNING

Has English literature a place in the teaching of English as a second-language? The question is relevant in view of the fact that there are educationists in the country who make much of the concept of English as a 'library language'. By treating English as a library language they minimise its importance in India and tend to see it as a language which will help students and others who seek information on one subject or another from English books. That is to say, English as a second-language in India need be taught only to serve as a useful medium for gleaning information, and information alone.

The place of English in India, as we have seen in the first chapter of this book, is unlike that of any other foreign language, say, Russian or French. It is in this context that we have asserted that English is a second language in India and not a foreign language. The study of a second language aims at a fairly good command of the language for purposes of communication and does not, therefore, rule out a reading of the literature in the language.

The total process of learning a second-language involves far more than simply learning the forms of the language; it also involves a knowledge of the culture of those who speak the language. This is because effective communication in a second-language depends not only on a knowledge of how things are said but also on what is said. In the words of Charles C. Fries, "A thorough mastery of a language for practical communication with real understanding demands a systematic observation and recording of many features of the precise situations in which the varied sentences are used. Such a systematic observation and recording must be minute and sympathetic, not for the purpose of evaluation in terms of one's own practices, or of finding the 'quaint' customs, but in order to understand and to feel and to experience as fully as possible."[1]

More or less the same view is expressed by Albert Marckwardt too. He says: "For many years foreign language study...has been justified on the ground that proficiency in the language constitutes a key to the understanding of the culture of a country and the psychology and personality traits of its people. Today we continue to accept this premise, tempered only perhaps by the more conscious caveat that such cultural insights will be attained only if they occupy a prominent place among the language course objectives and if some way of implementing them can be carefully worked out."[2]

The study of English as a second-language is strengthened as a result of satisfactory cultural orientation on the part of the student. Such an orientation becomes easier through a reading of the literature in the language; for the language in which the literature is written reflects and reinforces the cultural patterns and value system of those who speak the language.

Apart from cultural orientation literature helps the student come to grips with the idiom of the language. More and more exposure to the language through its literature enables the student to understand the subtle differences between certain words and appreciate the hidden nuances of thought and style the idiom of the language is capable of.

According to John F. Povey the following are some of the general aims of the teaching of literature:

1. Literature will increase all language skills because literature will extend linguistic knowledge by giving evidence of extensive and subtle vocabulary usage and complex and exact syntax. It will often represent in a general way the style that can properly stand as a model for students...

2. Literature is a link towards that culture which sustains the expression of any language. American literature will open up the culture of this country (America) to the foreign student in a manner analogous to the extension of the native speaker's own awareness of his own culture...

3. We must acknowledge the indefinable, though all-important, concept that literature gives one awareness and human insight...

4. Literature may guide a few more gifted students towards their own creativity by example derived from their reading of successful writers. There is already fascinating evidence of a second-language literature in English from several countries across the world, especially India and Nigeria.[3]

Certainly reading literature with interest and pleasure should be within everybody's reach. So, everyone studying English as a second-language should be encouraged to take an interest in its literature in the language. This can be done by a careful selection of material that has been properly graded and that suits the linguistic capacities of the student.

The question that should engage our attention is not whether English literature has a place in the teaching of English in India, but how best we can include a meaningful programme of English literature in the language course and what this programme should consist of. Perhaps it is not necessary that in the lower levels of teaching English as a second-language, literary forms—poetry, the novel and the drama—need be given a place. But at the pre-degree and undergraduate levels students should be encouraged to read literature.

A meaningful programme of English literature should consist of not only literary selections but also literary forms such as poetry, the novel and the drama. Literary selections in this context should be regarded as 'artifacts of culture' and not merely as a means for vocabulary improvement or grammar study. But care should be taken to see that the selections do not go over the head of the student; for if he is driven to look up the dictionary frequently for lexical items and idiomatic expressions which he is not familiar with, he is likely to lose interest in reading the selections, and the purpose will be defeated. That is to say, while we recognise the importance of literature in an English language course, we should also recognise the need for including in the syllabus such selections as those that will not cause any great linguistic difficulty to the student. This is, however, not a difficult proposition; what we have to do is to adapt the selections by means of simplifying syntactic structures and by means of vocabulary control. Also, we should see that we select material that will generally suit the academic level and maturity of the student. Such a graded selection is possible if our textbook editors are not haphazard in their approach.

The teaching of English in India began its attention to literature with the reading of such classical writers as Shakespeare, Thackerary, Dickens, etc. There was even a case of Carlyle's *Abbot Samson* having been prescribed for a language course at the old Intermediate level. Books like *Abbot Samson* will not be read with pleasure and understanding. There is, however, every justification for recommending simplified versions of classics to students at the Secondary and Higher Secondary stages. Shakespeare's plays may be prescribed for analytical reading at the under-graduate level. What is required is a moderate dose of literature, and not a total ban on the study of literature.

Here again caution has to be exercised in the selection of the novels, short stories, plays and poems that are to be included in a language course. One special aspect of language difficulty is the dialogue in novels, short stories and plays; dialogue in dialect form which is full of colloquial idioms may cause difficulties. It is better that books containing dialogues, overwhelmingly dialectal and colloquial, are left out.

Though the primary objective of the student reading literary selections and works in an English language course is to develop insights into the culture of the native speakers of the language, yet poems, novels and short stories by Indian writers in English and selections from their writings may also be included in the syllabus. Since these works deal with situations familiar to the student, they will be easily appreciated by him. Moreover, his reading of literary works by both Indian and English writers will give him an opportunity to take note of the cultural differences between the native and non-native speakers of English and will enable him to make a contrastive study of two different traditions. The feasibility of contrastive analyses has been recognised by linguists and language teaching experts. According to Marckwardt, "...it may be reasonably maintained that contrastive cultural analyses are equally important in terms of the aims of language study."[4]

The most important thing is securing an interest in literature and encouraging voluntary reading. This can be achieved through careful selection. That is to say, the work that is prescribed for reading should evoke proper response in the student. Good, simple material though not first-rate, is likely to arouse interest whereas difficult material will create a distaste for literature.

The presentation of the work in class is most important in creating an interest in literature in the student. A work of fiction, for instance, should be presented in its entirety as quickly as possible. Perhaps dividing it into more or less self-contained episodes and treating each episode as the subject of a lesson can be one way of doing this. A good loud reading in class of certain key portions can also be thought of.

Introducing a play well can sometimes be a problem. A safe way is to plunge right into the dramatic situation by starting with a reading in parts. The teacher should, however, be able to convey as much meaning as possible by his reading. The presentation of the whole work may be followed by discussion. The teacher's role is crucial in making the details clearer and in directing the attention of students to the relevant parts of the text. The teacher may at first ask general questions and then work inwards to ask specific questions. Here the teacher need not work through the play in the order in which details lie on the pages of the text. Discussion based on the literary and cultural content of the text may sometimes get down to single words, but should never be allowed to turn out to be a language lesson. Once the discussion based on the details of the play is over, the teacher may direct the attention of students to the work as a whole again. This will result in a fuller appreciation of the work now that the play has been subjected to a detailed examination.

The method suggested above may be made applicable *mutatis mutandis* to the other forms of literature. However, it should be remembered that any kind of discussion a work is subjected to should depend on its characteristics. Each work is unique, and therefore, demands varied treatment. This saves literature lessons from being stereotyped, even when general principles of treatment remain the same.

The main points we have made in this chapter are that literature should not be excluded from the syllabus for teaching English as a second- language and that a meaningful programme of English literature as well as Indian literature in English, properly graded to suit the level of students' comprehension, has certain definite advantages which not only include cultural orientation so necessary for the learning of a second- language but also enable students to get a sound exposure to good English. However, as Bruce Pattison points out, "Learning to read literature must be carefully distinguished from studying it."[5] What he means is that though teaching English as a second-language should take into account creation of interest in literature in students, yet the language course should not at any rate be turned into a literature course. There is perhaps the possibility that the interest aroused in literature in language students will make them go on to the study of literature. This is good in itself, but should not be the objective of the second-language teacher, for the teacher "who encourages students to run before they can walk risks rote learning instead of the development of genuine capacity to deal with literature."[6]

References

1.   Fries, Charles C., *Teaching and Learning English as a Foreign Language,* Ann Arbor, 1945, p. 57

2.   Marckwardt, Albert, "The Cultural Preparation of the Teacher of English as a Second Language" in *Theory and Practice in English as a Foreign Language,* Ann Arbor, 1963, p. 1

3.   Povey, John F., "Literature in TESL Programmes: the Language and the Culture" in *Teaching English as a Second Language,* (edited by Harold B. Allen and Russell N. Campbell), Bombay: Tata McGraw-Hill, 1972, p. 187

4.   op. cit. p. 1

5.   Pattison, Bruce, "The Literature Lesson" in *Teaching English as a Second Language.* p. 195

6.   Pattison, Bruce, ibid., p. 198

For Further Reading

1.   Lemer, L.D., *English Literature: an Interpretation for Students Abroad*, O.U.P., 1955
2.   Moody, H.L.B., *The Teaching of Literature,* Longman: 1971
3.   Press, John (ed.), *The Teaching of English Literature Overseas,* Methuen, 1965

FOURTEEN

RETROSPECT AND PROSPECT

The importance of teaching English as a second-language in India cannot be minimised. It is a 'source' language as well as a 'link' language. It has enriched our own languages; it enables us to have easy access to modern knowledge and helps us maintain contact and exchange ideas among ourselves within the country and with others in the outside world. These reasons alone should compel us to reorganise the teaching of it in India on scientific lines.

The Government of India is conscious of the imperative need for strengthening the teaching of English in India and has appointed Study Groups from time to time. These Groups have made a number of recommendations on policies and programmes, syllabi, methods and materials. The Regional Institutes of English and the Central Institute of English and Foreign Languages too have made their contributions. All the same no tangible success has so far been achieved in the implementation of the policies and programmes recommended by the Study Groups.

The reasons for non-implementation are many. One of them is the shortage of well-trained, fully qualified teachers of English in schools and colleges. A second reason is that teaching methods, classroom behaviour, relationships and motivation, about which so much excellent writing has been produced in the educational world in the last few years, have been completely ignored. A third reason is the non-availability of graded textbooks written and brought out for use at different stages of the educational system. The oral or direct method has been introduced and the structural approach based on Stannard Allen's Living English Structure has been adopted; yet no progress seems to have been achieved. The reason is again shortage of trained staff. The handful of available trained staff have been unhelpful; they have been shy of giving demonstration lessons to their untrained colleagues and of thus popularising effective teaching methods.

Apart from the above reasons there have been other factors too that are responsible for our failure in the successful implementation of any worthwhile English teaching programme. The frequent changes in governmental policy towards the teaching and learning of English, the indecisiveness of the State Education Departments as regards policies and programmes, non-availability of facilities and resources for reform and reorganisation, and ill-equipped institutions are some of these factors. It is no exaggeration to say that no effective teaching of English is being done at present in schools and colleges situated in the rural areas. Perhaps the situation is different in the urban areas; for here there are well- established English-medium schools to which are sent the children of the upper-class and middle-class urban elite.

The attitudes of teachers in general are yet another factor that stands in the way of effective English language teaching in India. These attitudes are a legacy of the past and have become part of traditional thinking and practice, and can be overcome only with proper training and motivation. L.A. Hill in an article entitled "The Mythology of English Teaching" speaks of these attitudes as myths and exposes their meaninglessness. Of the myths listed by Hill, two are worth mentioning; these are: undue emphasis on the teaching and appreciation of English literature and the teaching of textbooks that students cannot easily cope with; a belief that grammatical analysis helps students write better English. Hill's comment is that no student can respond to literature unless he has a good command of words and grammatical patterns and that the student learns to use the language grammatically through guided practice more quickly and easily than by theory and analysis.[1]

Approaches, techniques and methodologies continue to be the same old ones. For instance, lecturing has been an age-old technique in colleges and universities and teachers still adhere religiously to lecturing. They believe that courses should be more literature-oriented than language-oriented; they do not teach students how to speak and write English; there is neither oral practice nor written work in class; tutorial work is neglected; regular periodic tests for the purpose of evaluating the progress and achievement of students are not held. The teachers' excuse for the scant attention they pay to tutorial work and tests is that classes are large and that students do not have any interest in assignments, composition exercises and tests.

What happens in colleges is only an extension of what happens in schools. In schools the emphasis is certainly on language, and not on literature; yet no effective teaching is done. It is mainly the dearth of competent teachers, specially trained to teach English as a second-language, and the lack of teaching aids and materials that account for the present pitiable state of affairs in schools. The teachers in colleges find in this an excuse for their poor handling of English classes; they say that the teaching of English in colleges is not effective because the school-leavers come to the college with little or no English.

Having mentioned some of the major factors that have had the most deleterious effect on English teaching in India over the years, we may suggest that the remedy lies in getting down to grassroots and in concentrating on methodologies in the six years between the Fifth Standard and the Tenth Standard. It is desirable that English teaching commences from the Fifth Standard as at that level the language can be taught by Secondary School teachers who alone (and not primary School Teachers too) need be trained in English teaching. With the availability of trained teachers, new syllabi, properly graded for each Standard, for the students to proceed gradually from simple to difficult and from difficult to more difficult patterns of sentences and to learn newer and newer words to improve their expressiveness, may be introduced. New methodologies with emphasis on the four-language skills will have to be initiated both in schools and in colleges. These methodologies should depend on techniques that will motivate students to learn English and to enjoy learning it.

What is most needed is a change in the attitudes of our teachers—a change that will make them aware that lecturing is not the only teaching technique and that unless they are teaching literature as such they are teaching English as a second-language. This awareness will have to be accompanied by their preparedness to employ new methodologies, approaches and techniques for imparting instruction in the four language skills and for creating in students an interest in both English and its literature.

Reference

1.   Hill, L.A., "The Mythology of English Teaching" in *Teaching English*, Vol. VI, No. 4, August 1961

For Further Reading

1.   Gokak, V.K., *English in India: Its Present and Future,* Bombay: Asia Publishing House, 1964

2.   *Report of the Study Group on Teaching of English,* New Delhi: Ministry of Education and Youth Services, Government of India, 1971

3.   *The Study of English in India,* New Delhi: Ministry of Education, Government of India, 1967.